Maria Barnas
Michele Bazzoli
Dagmar Bosma
Lara Almarcegui
Yana Naidenov

speed up these branches reaching
you know
and they will crawl with us
through the mud
we will pick up
signals from the weed
that is not strangling
but sending messages to find a way
out this way this way slow down
speed up slow slower
we will arrive one day
at a place where time does not
strangle what
what?
who we think we
what we { } who we
who do we think
we are

loop from beginning

Maria Barnas

read out loud walking around a tree you trust

as nettles rush up
as curled leaves fold out
as stems stretch stretch stems
and brambles find a way
through the lime green
forest watery grass
as strangle weed threads
a life along the nettles
a defence line
from a time when boats
were expected to stay
where they could not sail
and boots to turn
where they could not wade

as this line is still
{ }

as we reach for
{ }

and some freedom yields

seeing a plant grow so
fast-forward that its stems
creep like caterpillars
antlers winding and weaving
along where they need to { }
and we see that a reason why
we separate
plants from animals
is a narrow sense of men's
narrowing timelines

slow down the animal and it will be
tree
slow down the beast
it is me

Michele Bazzoli

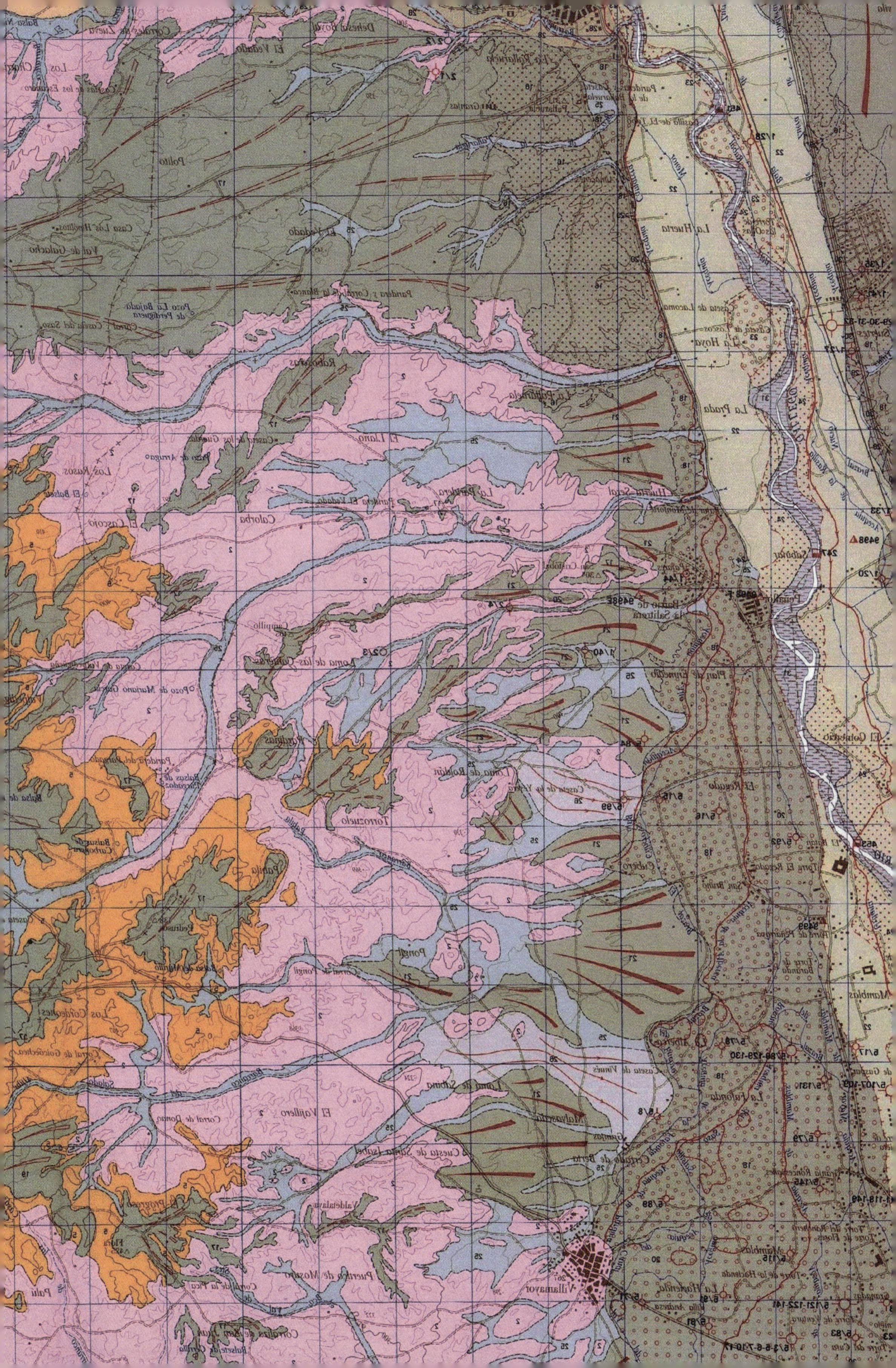

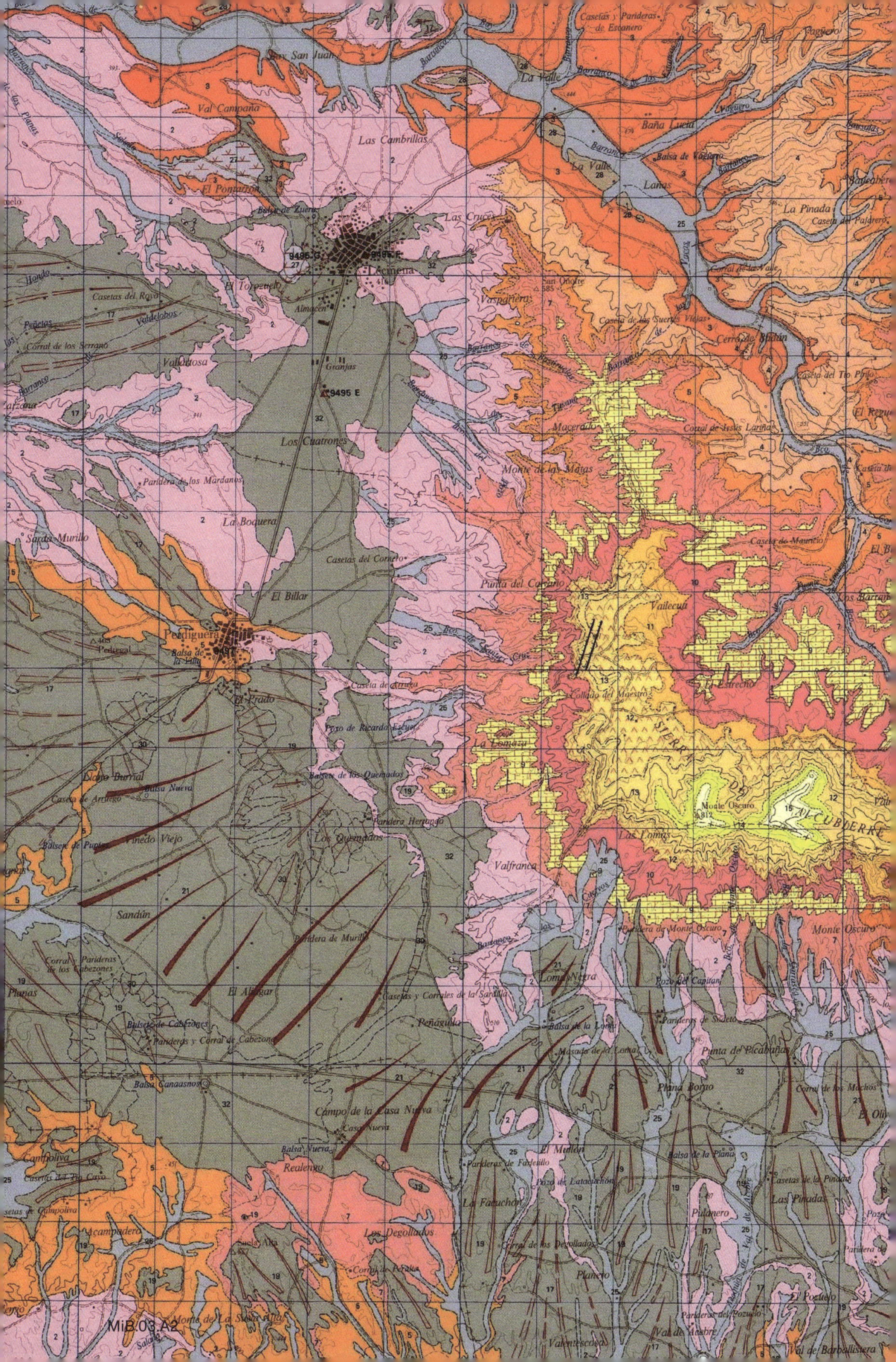

San Juan
Val Campaña
Las Cambrillas
El Pomatón
La Valle
La Valle
Lanas
Las Cruces
Vasparieras
Baña Lucía
Balsa de Vázqué
La Pinada
Caseta del Palúdero
Laguiero
Cerro de Madín
Caseta del Tío Prilo
Caseta de los Suertes Viejas
Corral de Isús Larina
El Billar
Pedriguera
El Prado
La Boquera
Los Cuatrones
Pardera de los Mardanos
Casetas del Corralo
Punta del Corano
Vallecua
Estrecho
Caseta de Mauricio
El Barranc
Los Barranc
Collado del Maestro
La Lomaza
Paso de Ricardo Escurín
Balsas de los Quemados
Pardera Hergugú
Los Quemados
Monte Oscuro
Las Lomas
Valfranca
Sandún
Pardera de Murillo
Corral Parderas de los Cabezones
El Albésar
Casetas y Corrales de la Sardilla
Peñagüda
Balsa de la Loma
Masada de la Loma
Pardera de Monte Oscuro
Monte Oscuro
Pozo del Capitán
Parderas de Sudeto
Punta de Picabuñas
Corral de los Machos
Olí
Plana Bonjo
Balsa Ganaasnos
Campo de la Casa Nueva
Casa Nueva
Balsa Nueva
Realengo
El Muñón
Parderas de Fadeullo
Pozo de Latauchón
Balsa de la Plana
Casetas de las Pinadas
Las Pinadas
Acampadero
La Fatuchón
Suelo Alto
Los Degollados
Corral de Peraña
Corral de los Degollados
Pulanero
Planero
El Postuelo
Parderas del Pozuelo
Val de Tauburi
Val de Barbollistera
Valenteschón

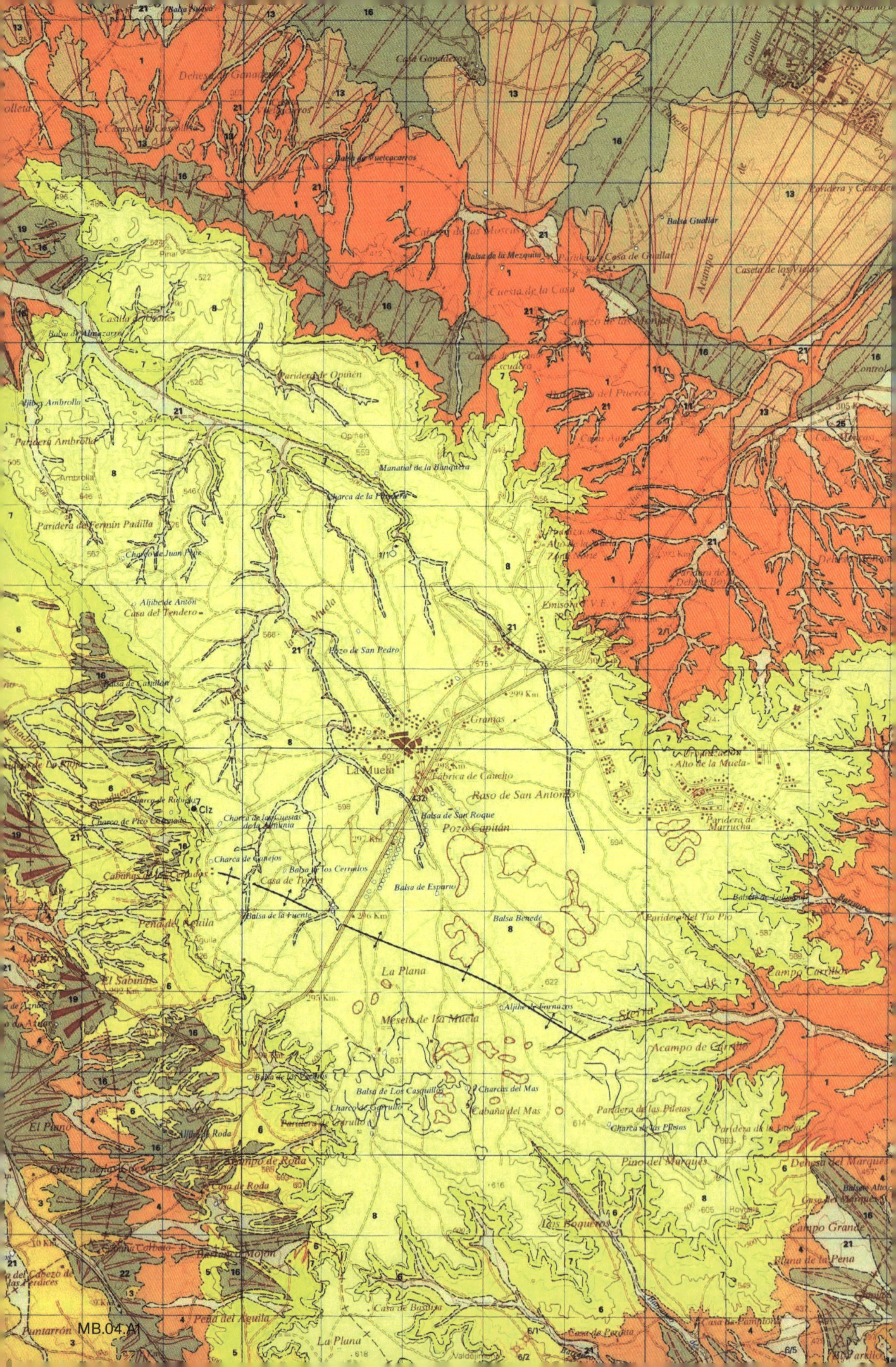

Dehesa de Ganados
Casa Ganaderos
Casilla de Casquillo
Balsa de Huelgacarros
Cabeza de las Moscas
Balsa de la Mezquita
Cuesta de la Casa
Balsa Guallar
Partidera y Casa de Guallar
Acampo
Caseta de los Viejos
Casilla de Oñones
Balsa de Almazarin
Partidera de Opiñen
Opiñen
Manantial de la Banquera
Charca de la Huerta
del Puerco
Cabezo de las Moscas
Partidera Ambrolla
Ambrolla
Partidera de Fermín Padilla
Charco de Juan Pérez
Aljibe de Antón
Casa del Tendero
Pozo de San Pedro
Muela
Balsa de Castillón
Alto Norte
Emisora V.H.F.
299 Km.
Granjas
La Muela
Fábrica de Caucho
Raso de San Antonio
Balsa de San Roque
Pozo Capitán
Urbanización Alto de la Muela
Partidera de Marrucha
Charca de las Cuestas de la Almunia
Charca de Rinaldo
Charco de Pico Calzado
Charca de Conejos
Cabañas de los Cerrudos
Casa de Toro
Balsa de los Cerritos
Balsa de Esparto
Balsa de la Fuente
Balsa Benedé
Partidera del Tío Pío
Balsera de Toledano
Peña del Águila
El Sabinar
La Plana
Meseta de la Muela
Aljibe de Tornacos
Sicieta
Acampo de Castillo
Campo Castillo
Balsa de las Peñas
Balsa de los Casquillos
Charcas del Mas
Charco de Gorrulla
Cabaña del Mas
Partidera de las Piletas
Partidera Gorrulla
Charca de las Piñas
Partidera de la Venta
Aljibe de Roda
Acampo de Roda
Casa de Roda
Pino del Marqués
Dehesa del Marqués
Casa del Marqués
Campo Grande
El Plano
Los Boqueros
Plana de la Peña
Cabezo de las Perdices
Balsa del Mojón
Peña del Águila
Casa de Basatía
Casa de Pezota
Casa de Pamplona
Puntarrón
La Plana
Valdeira
MB.04.A1

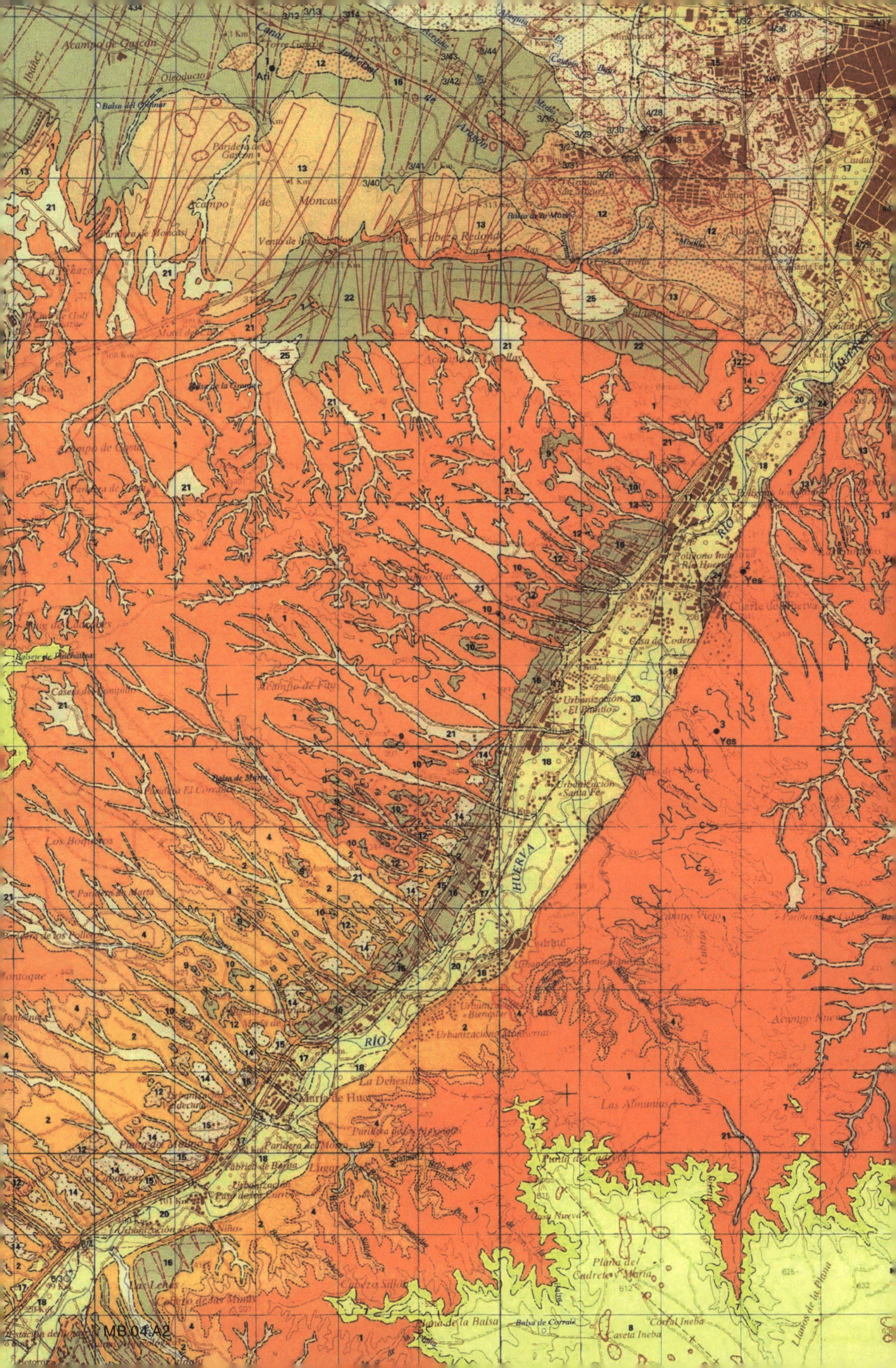

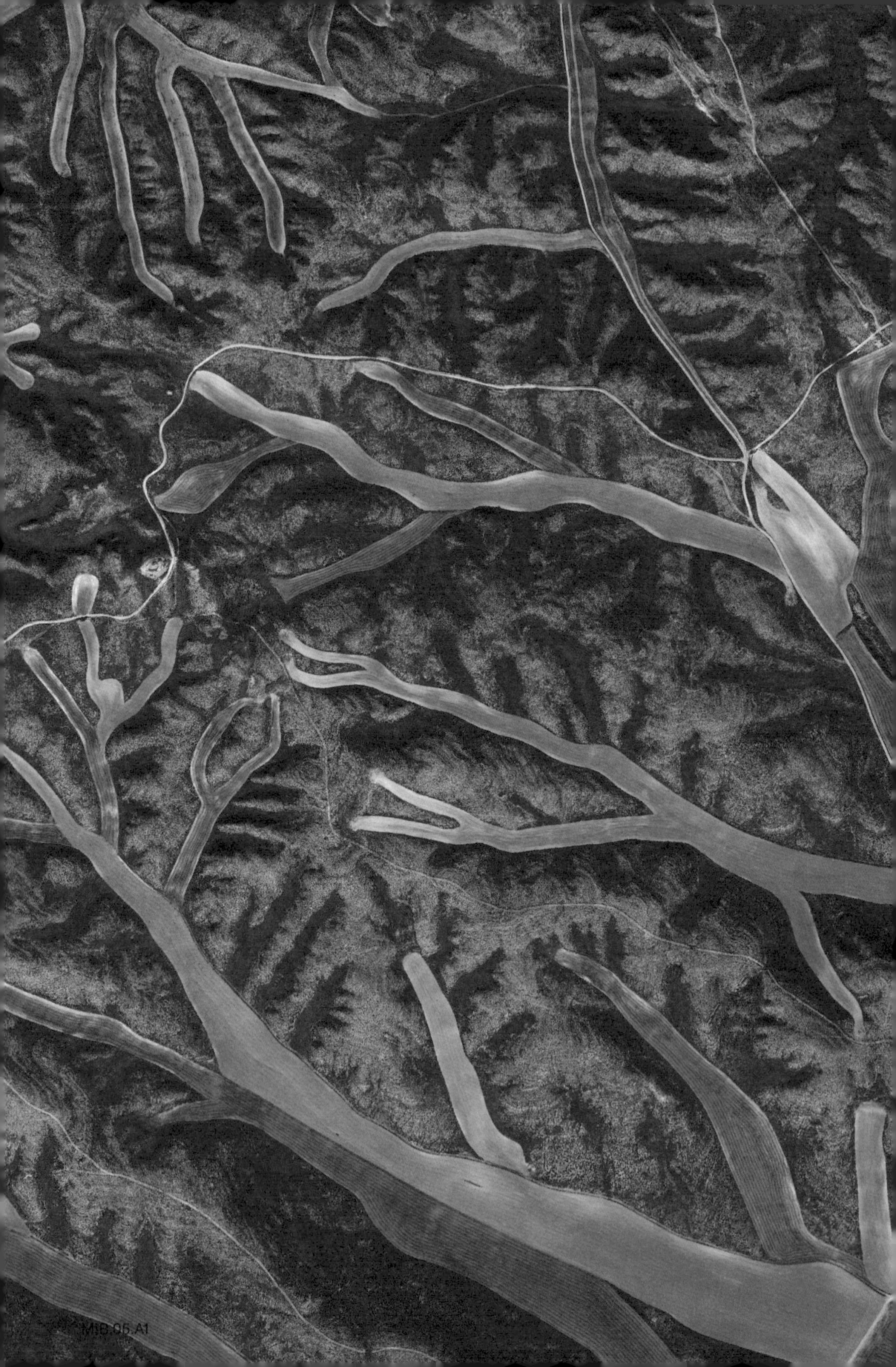
M18.05.A1

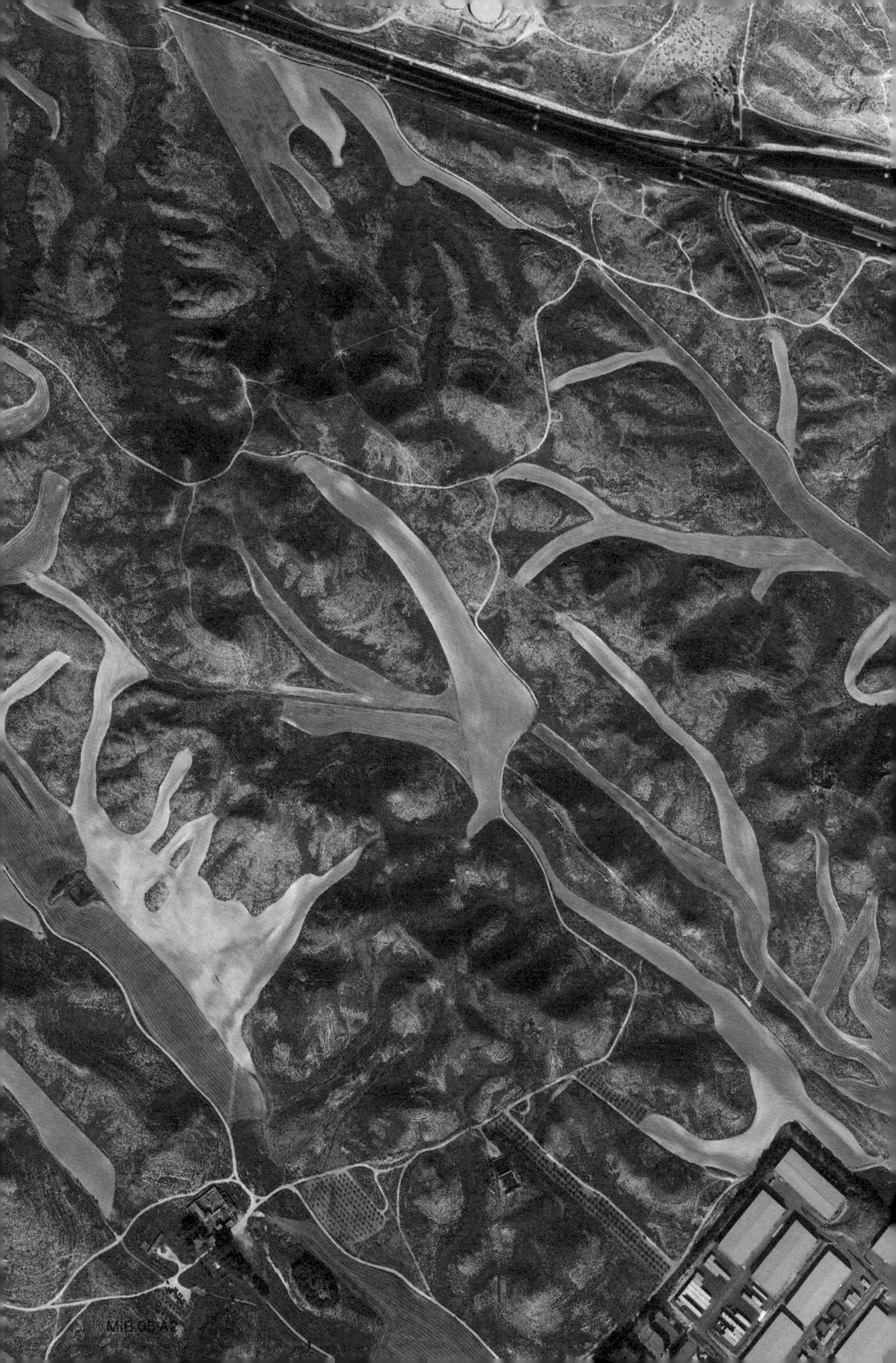

MiB 05 A2

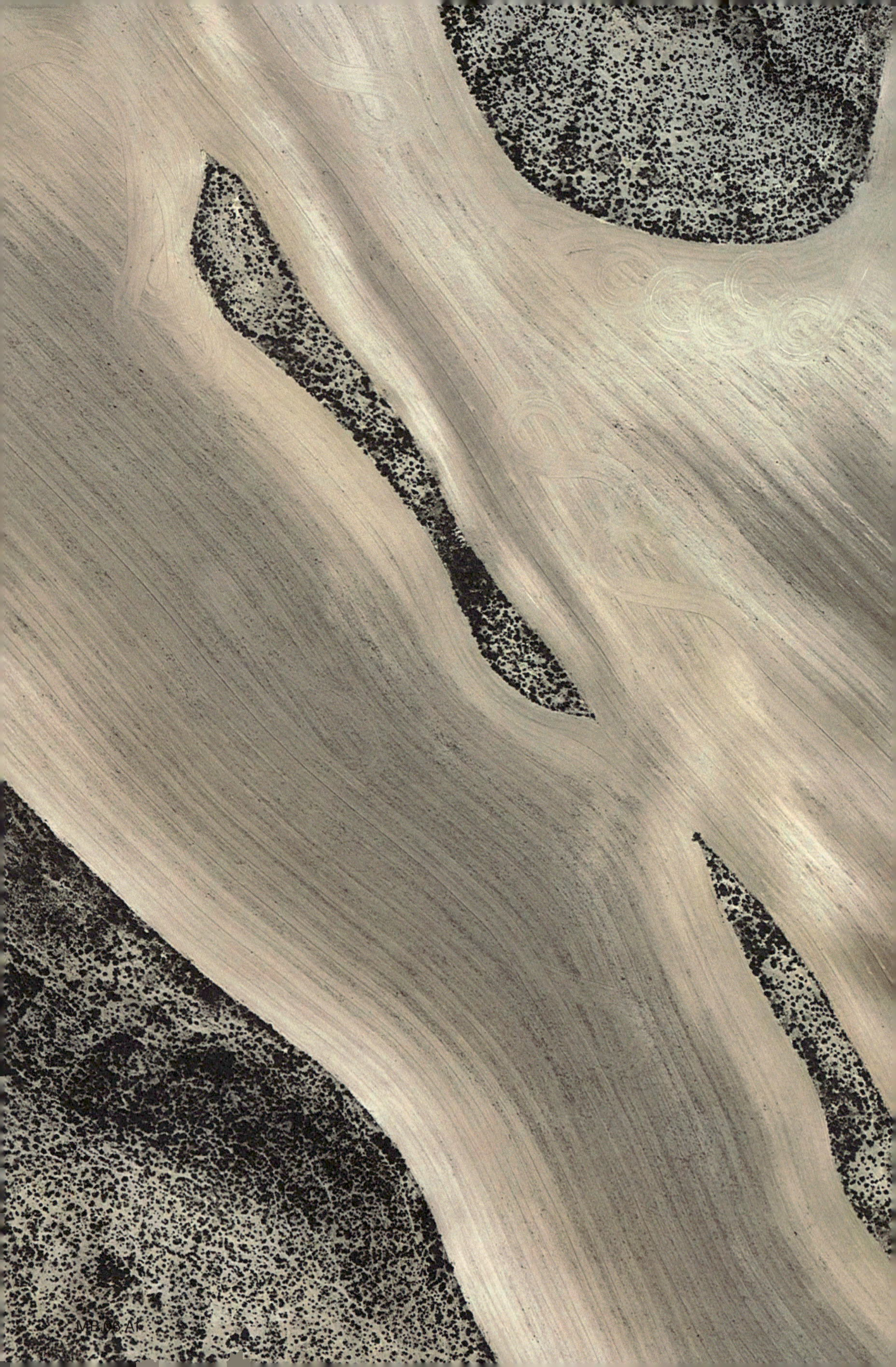

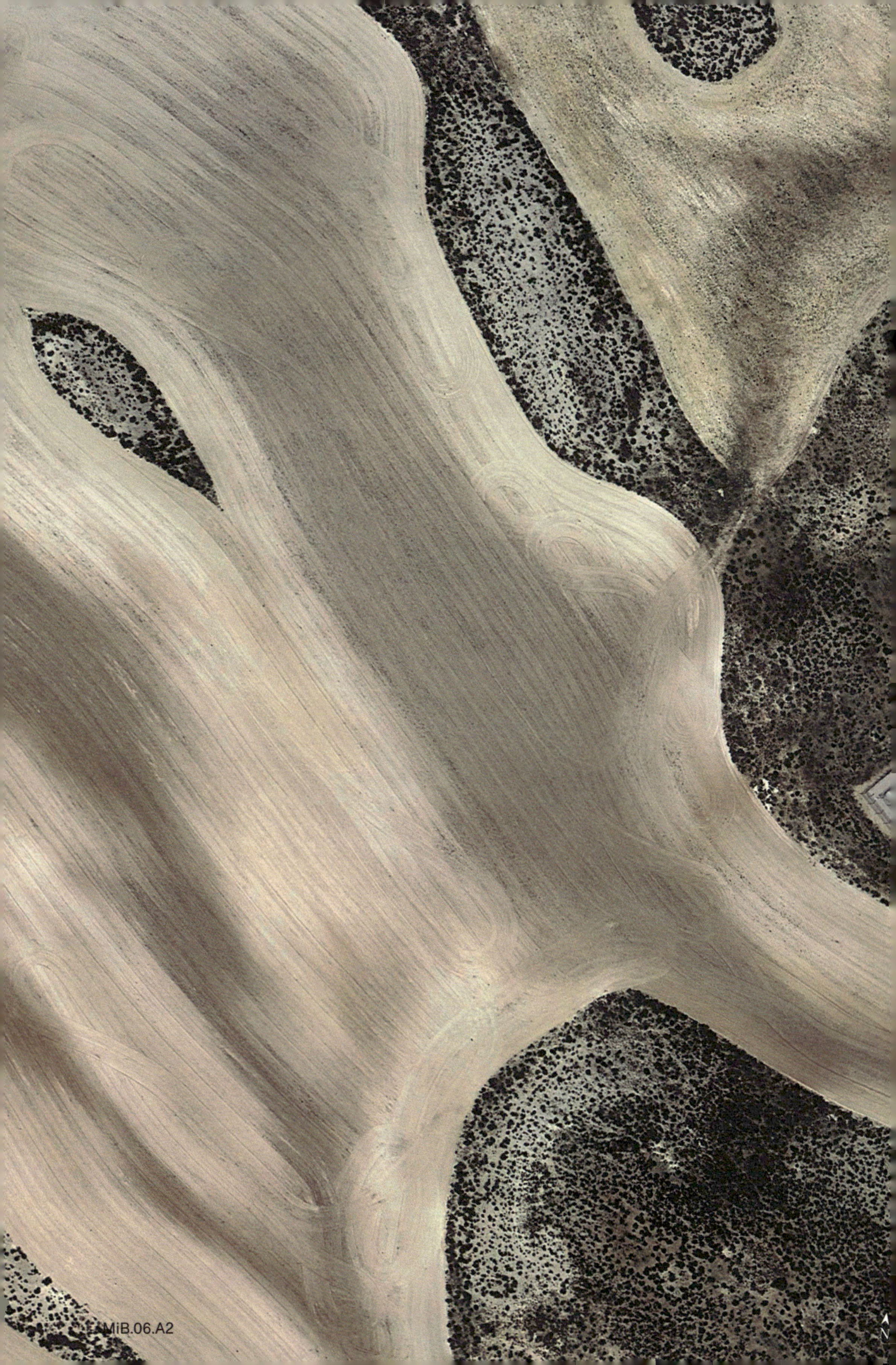
MiB.06.A2

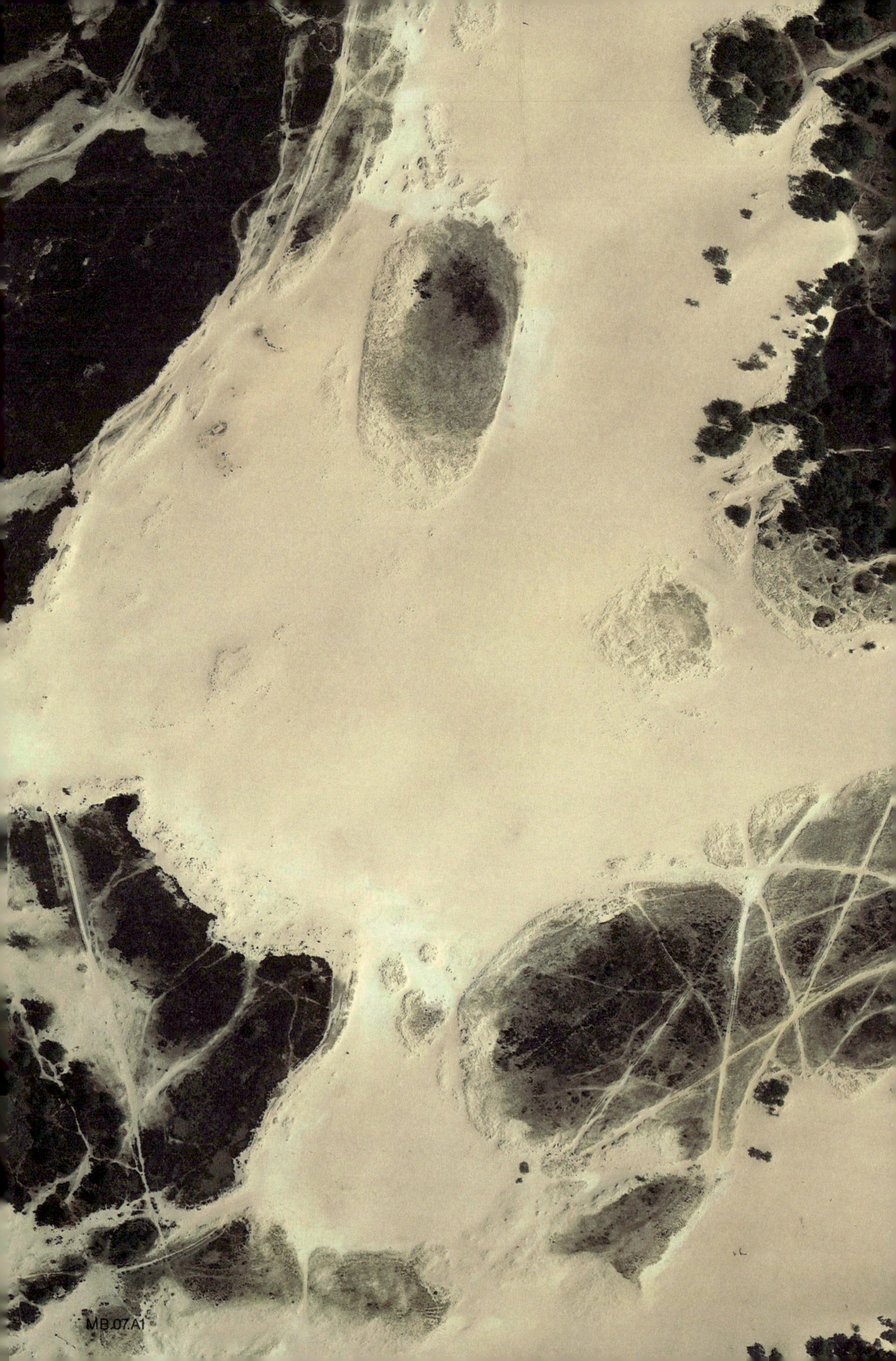
MB.07.A1

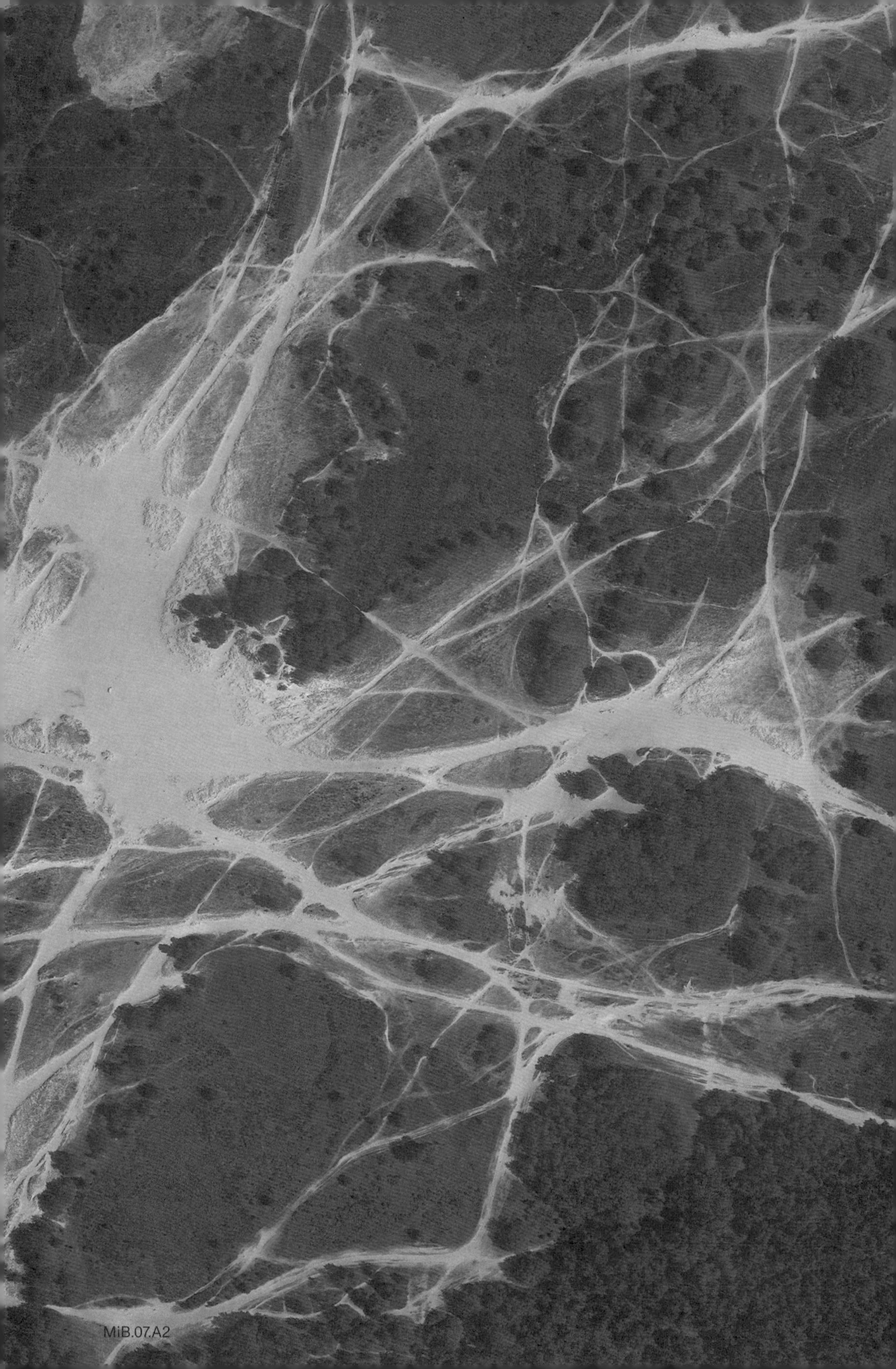
MiB.07.A2

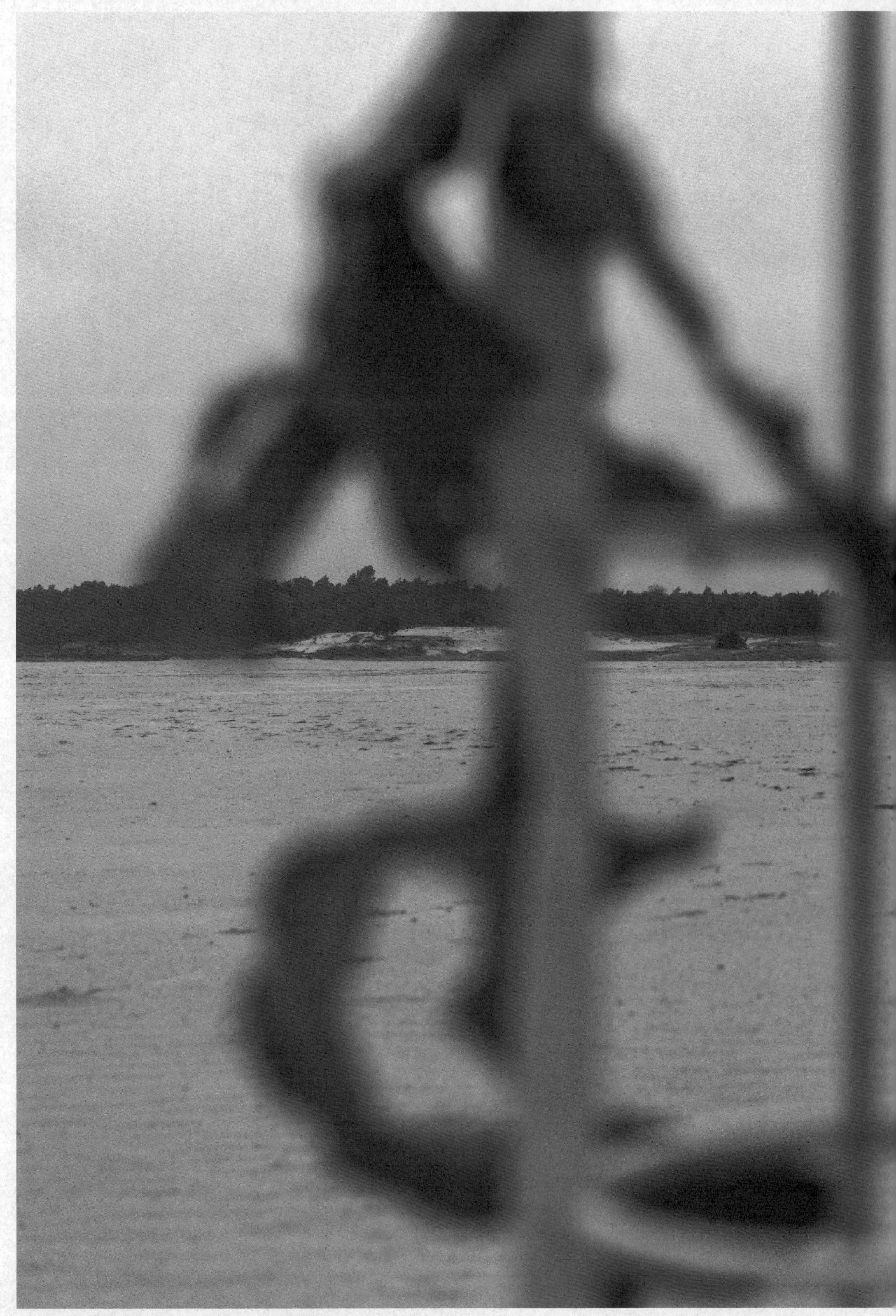
MiB.08.A1

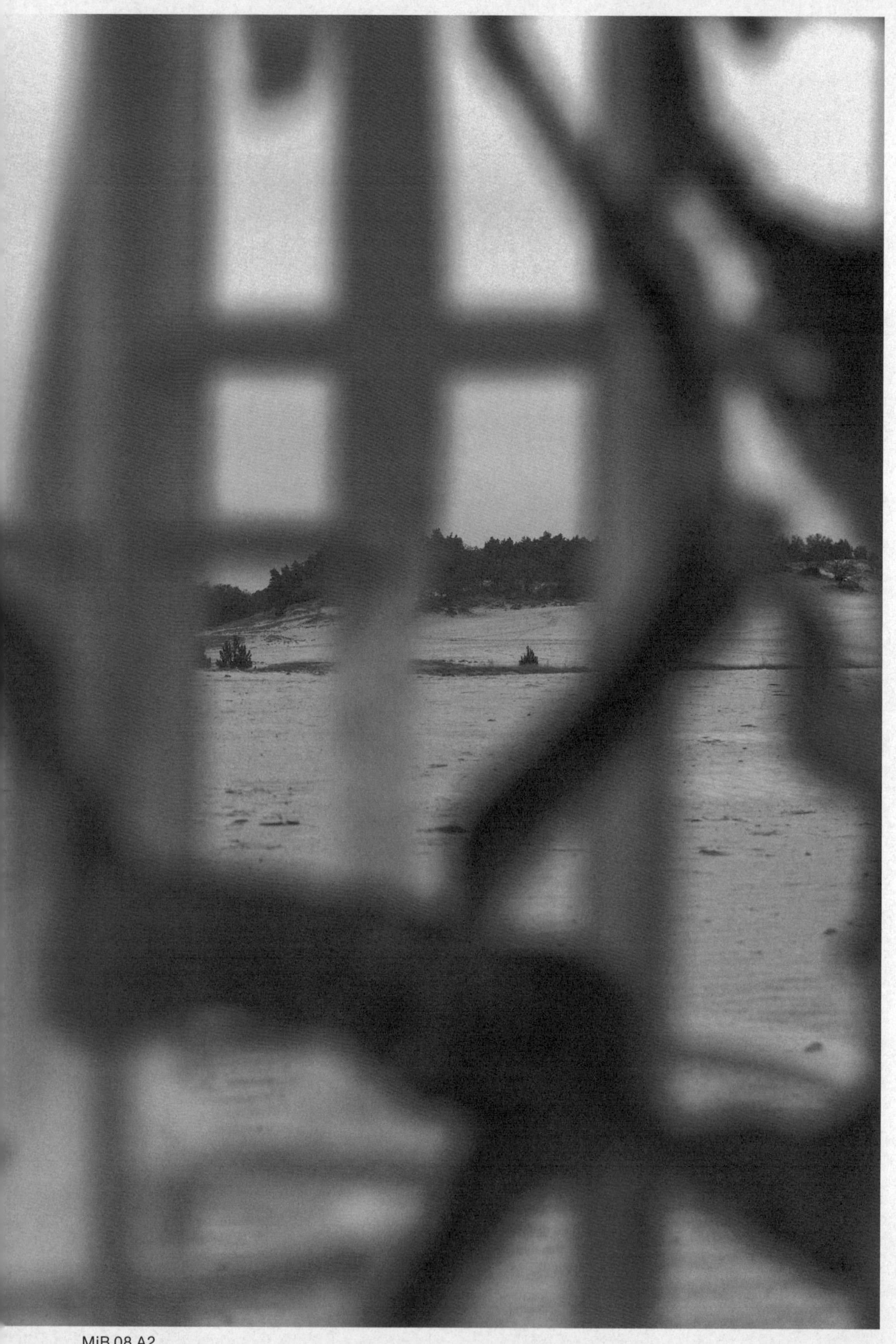

MiB.08.A2

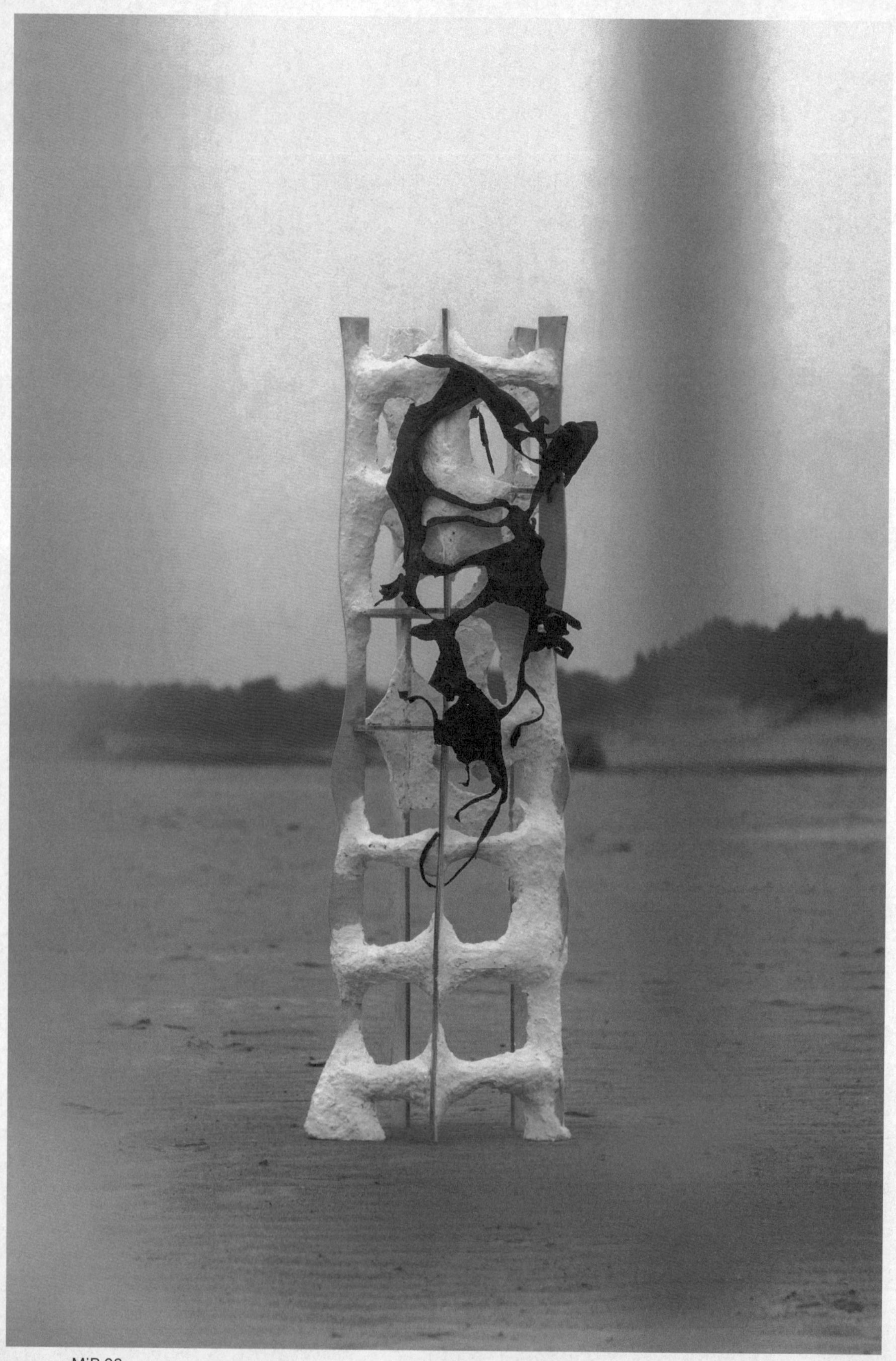

MiB.09

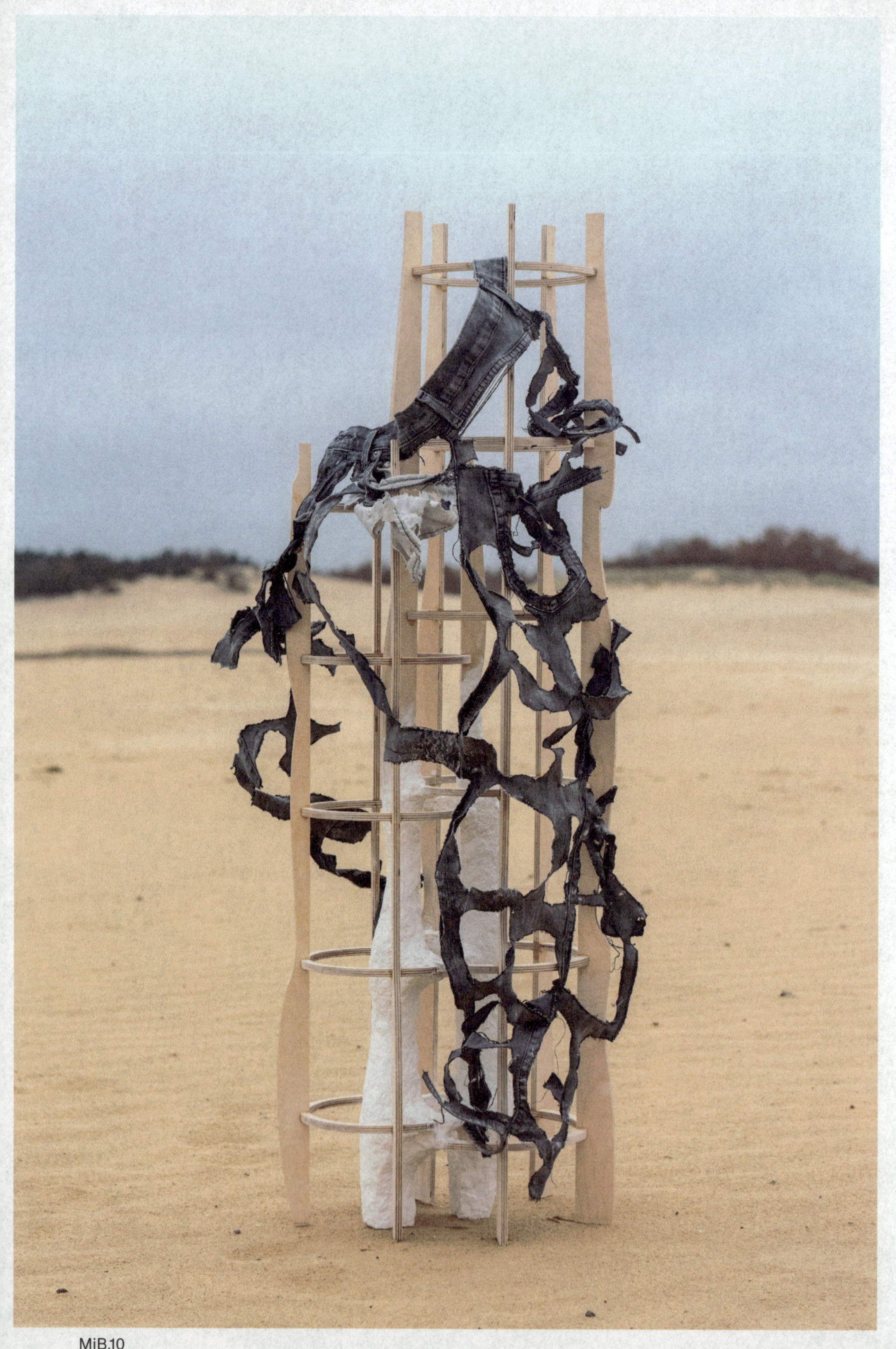

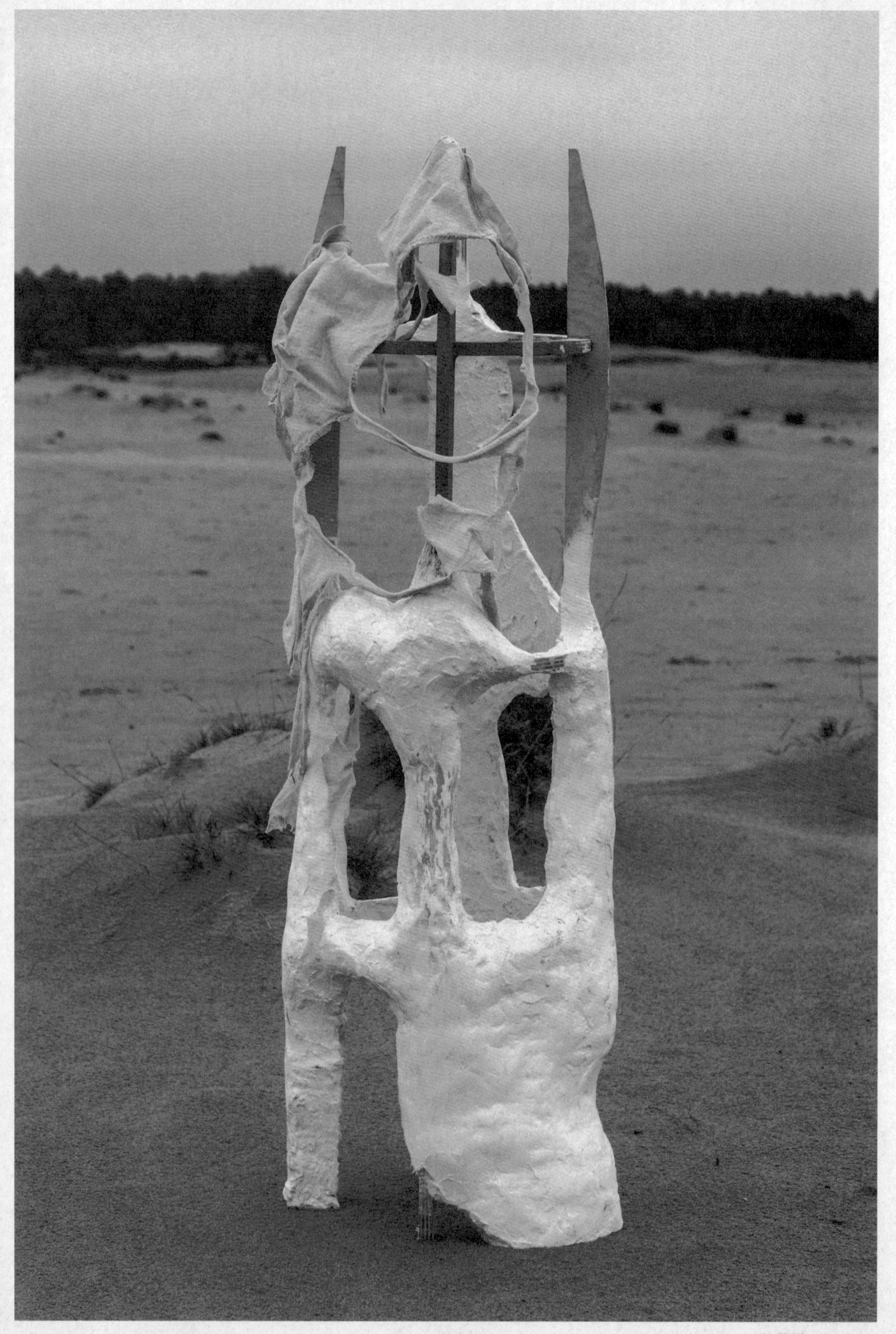

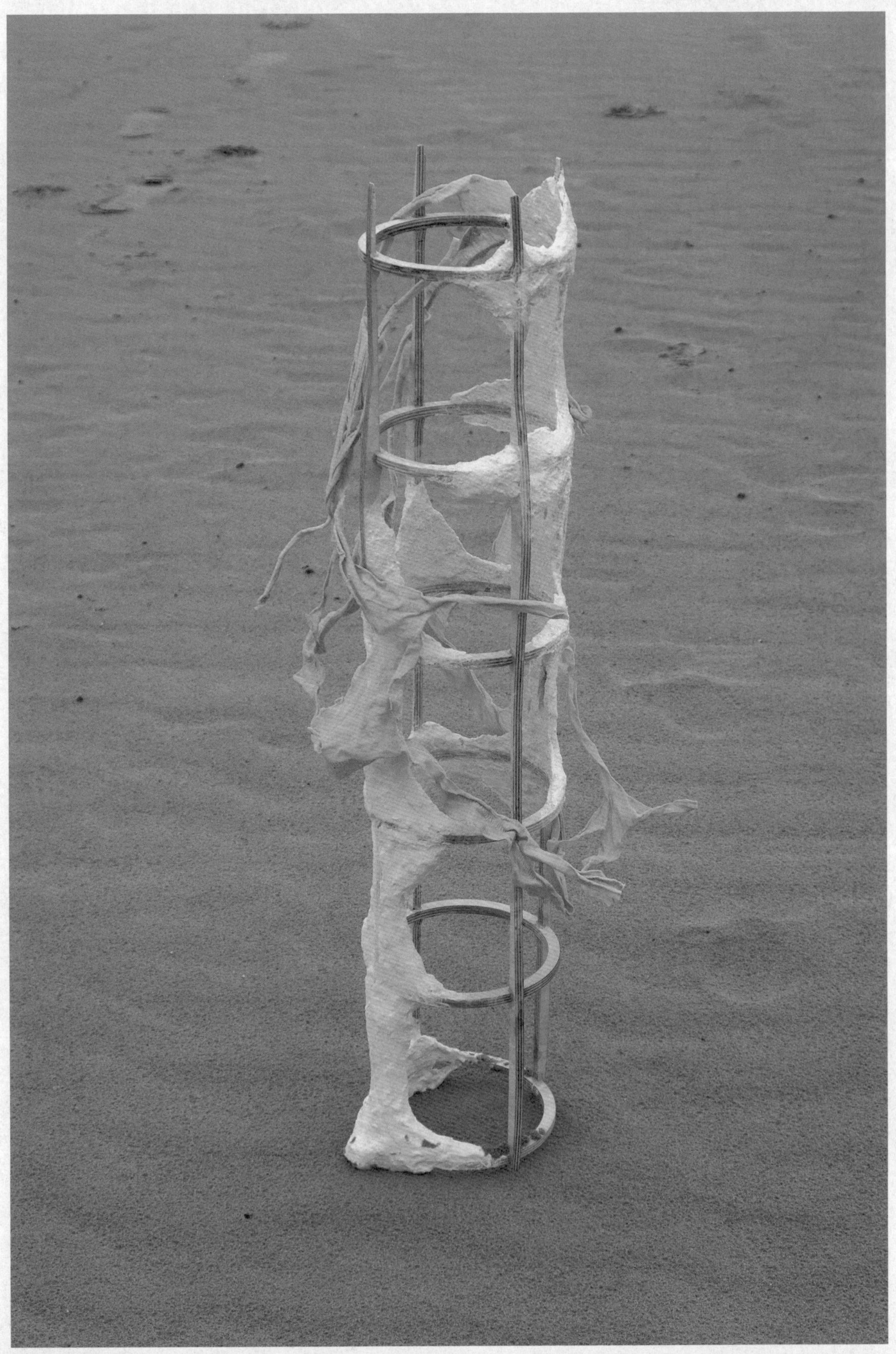

MiB.12

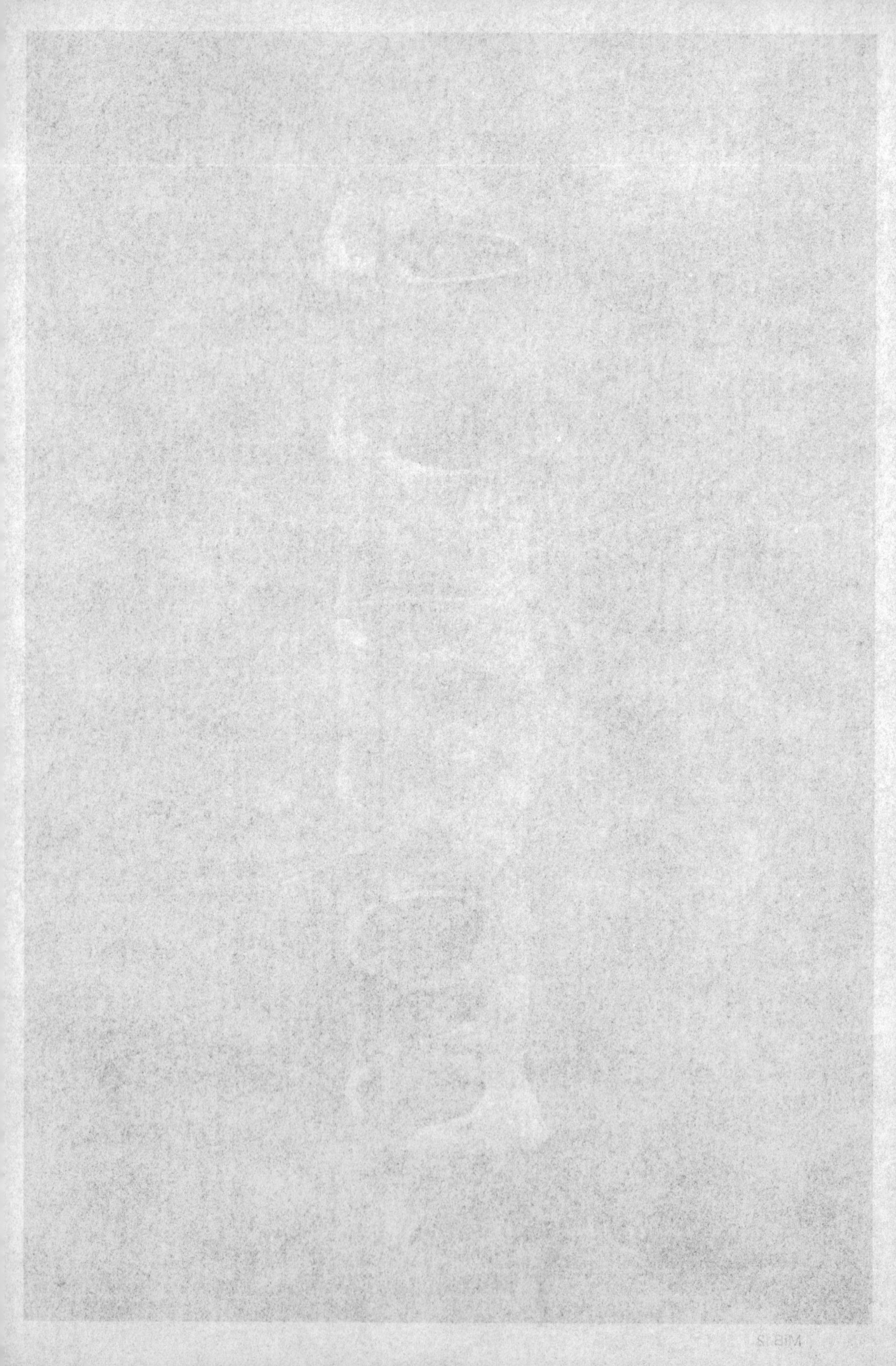

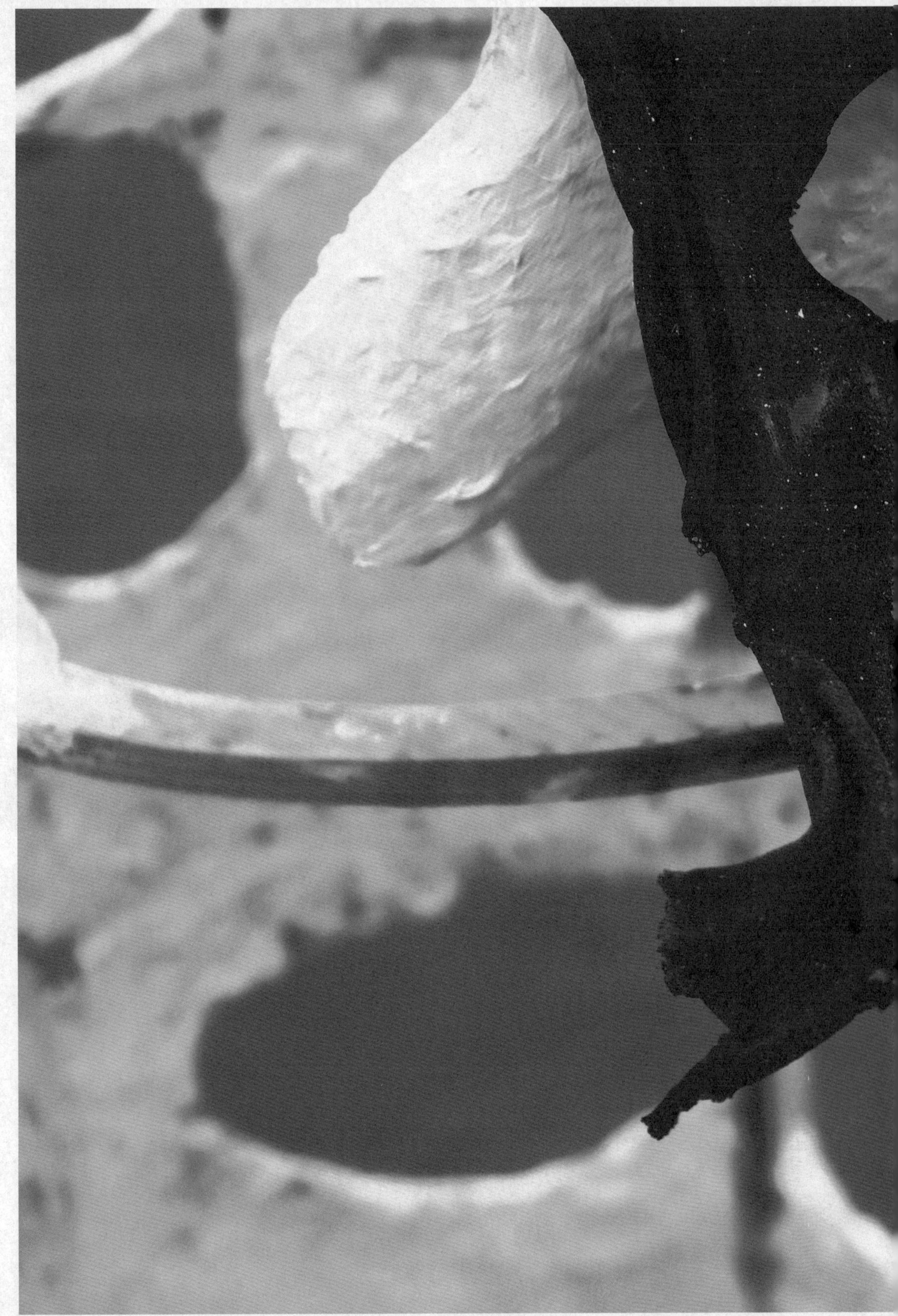

MiB.13.A1

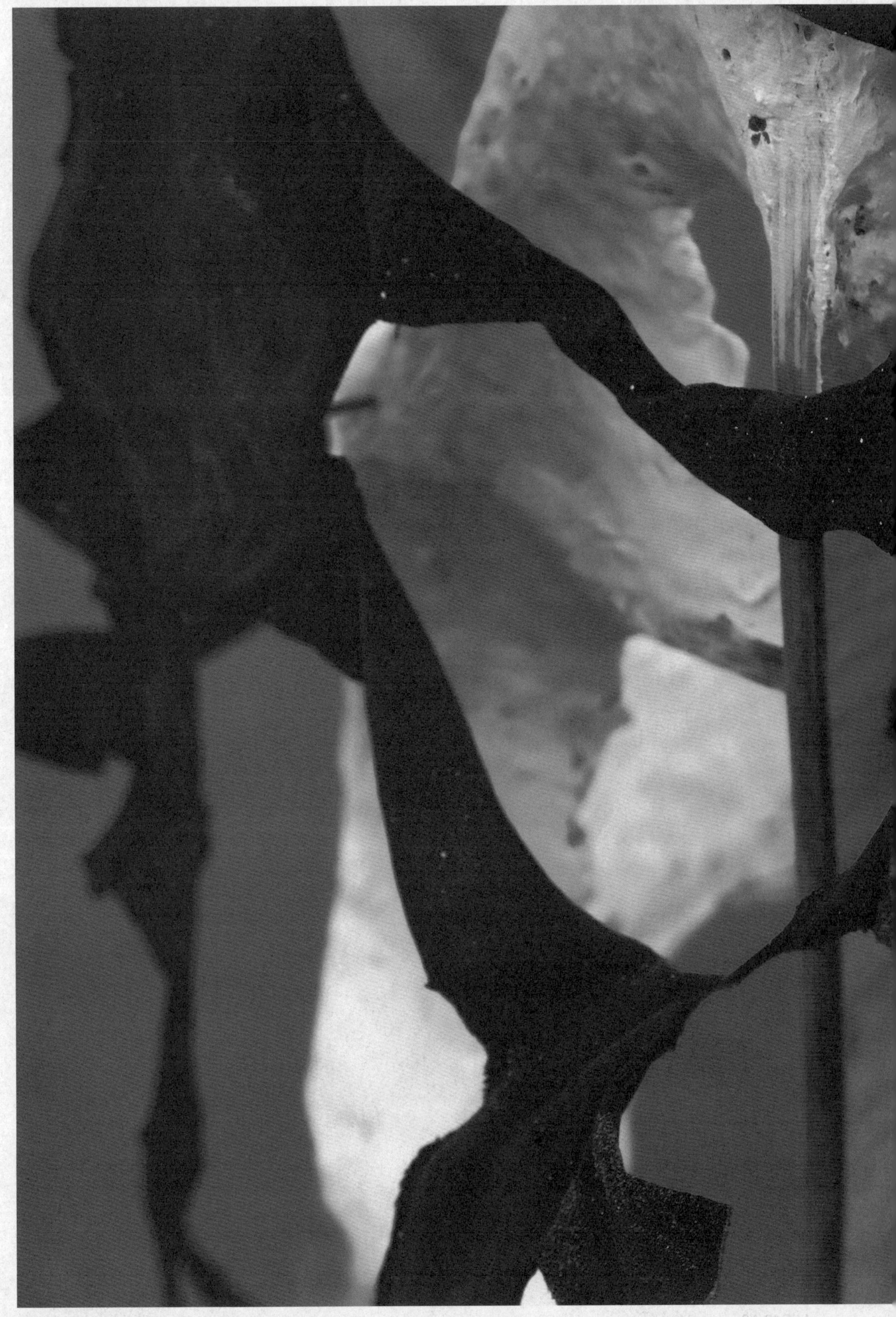

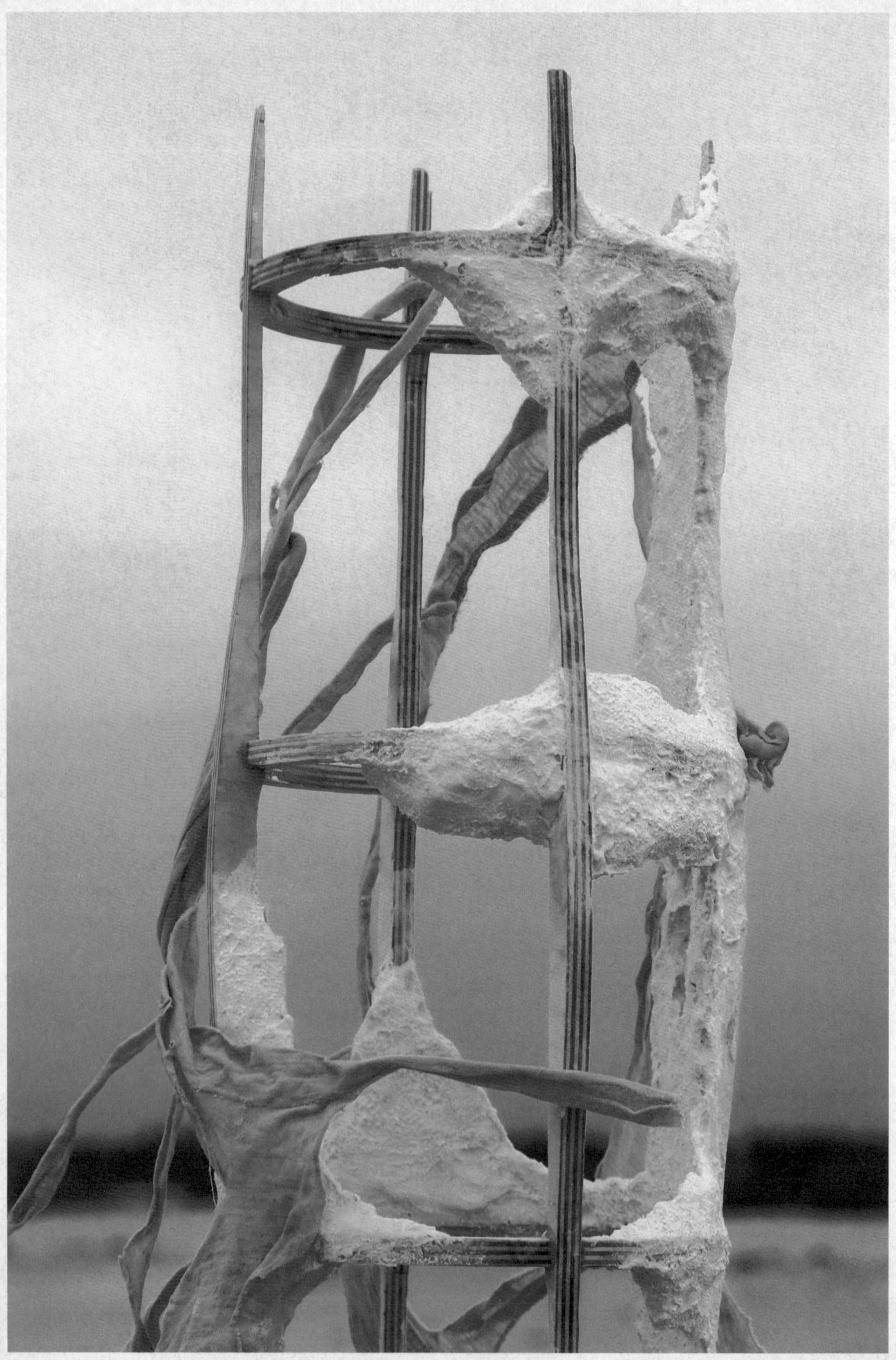

MiB.14

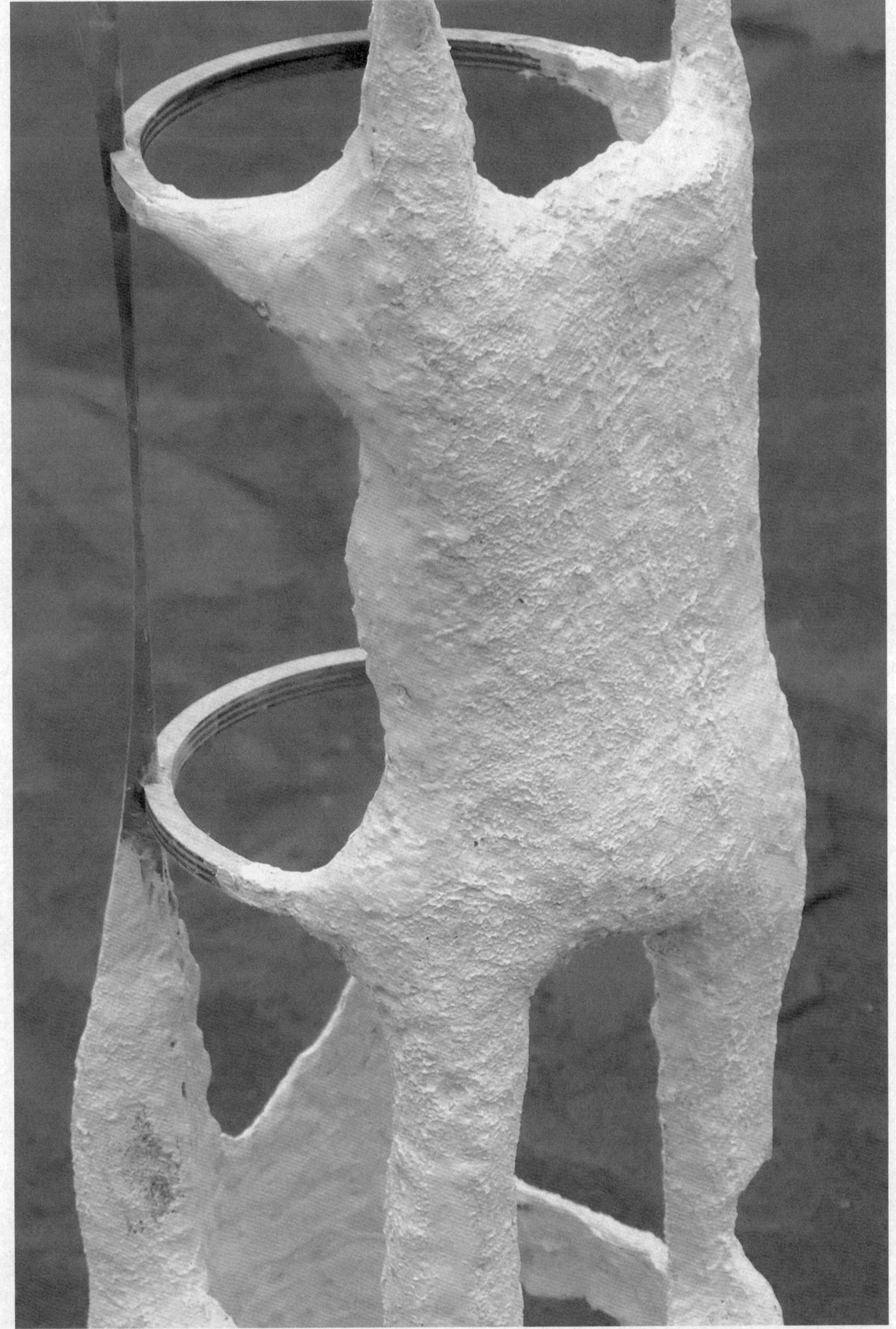

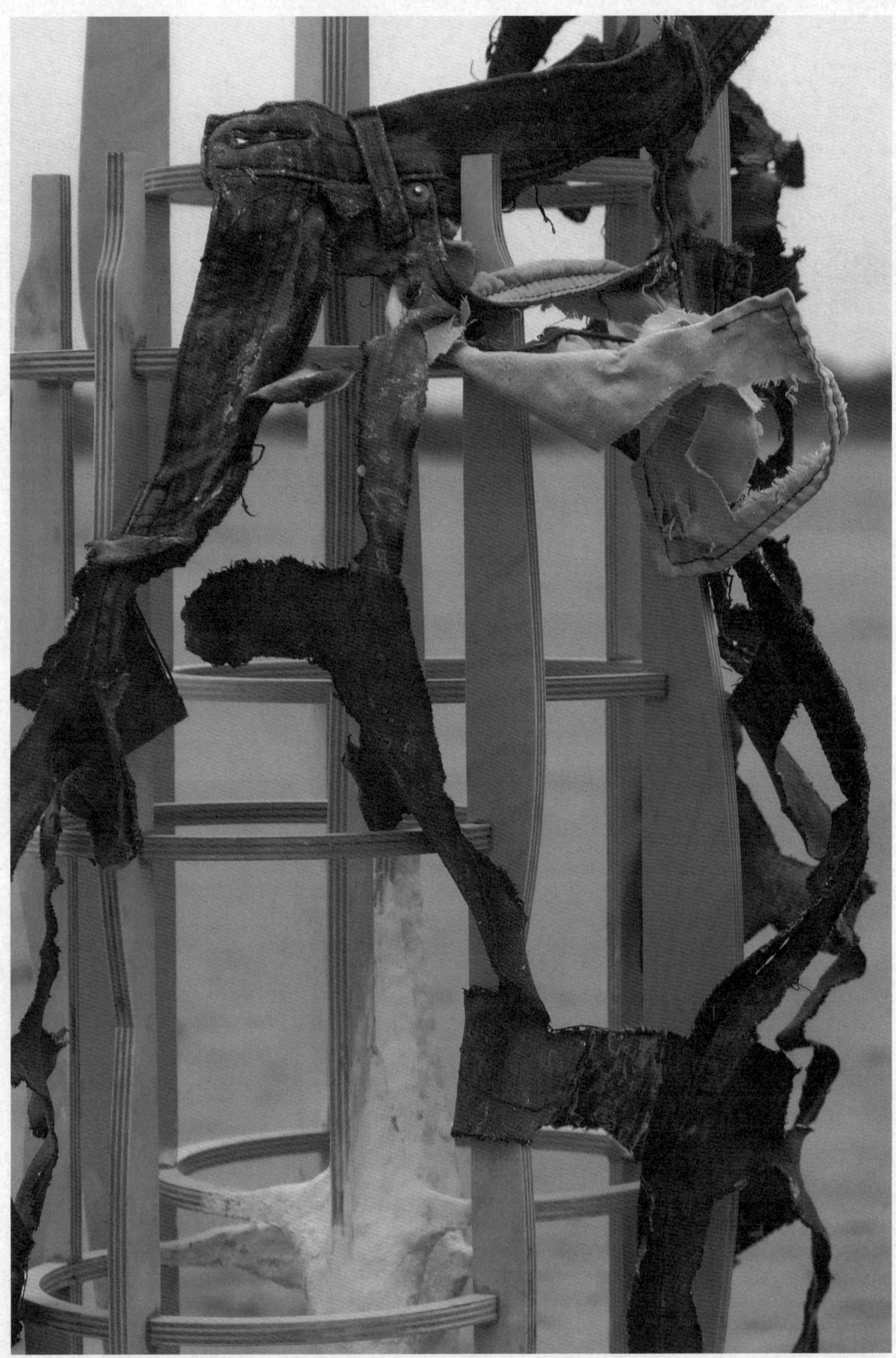

MiB.16

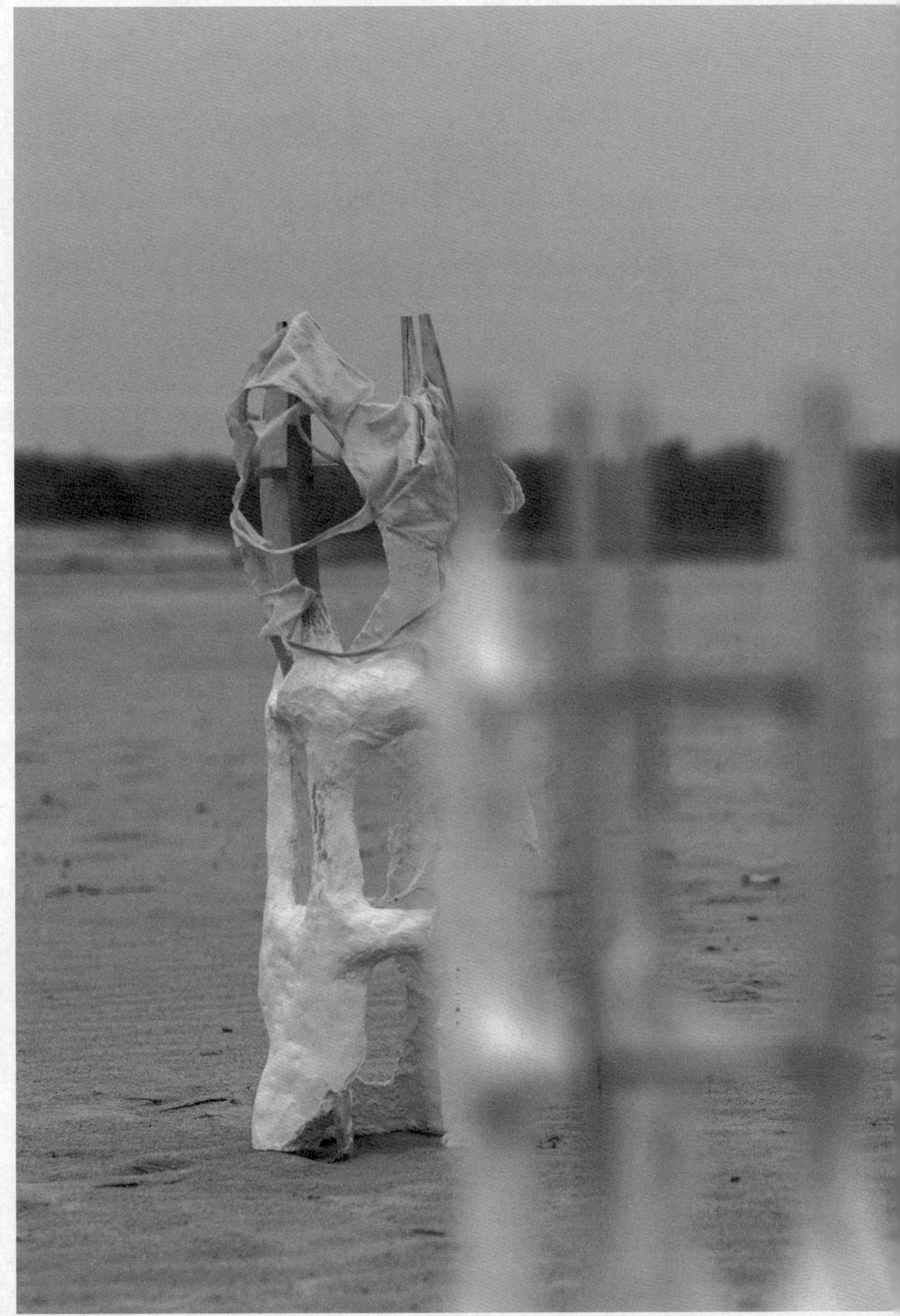

MiB.17.A1

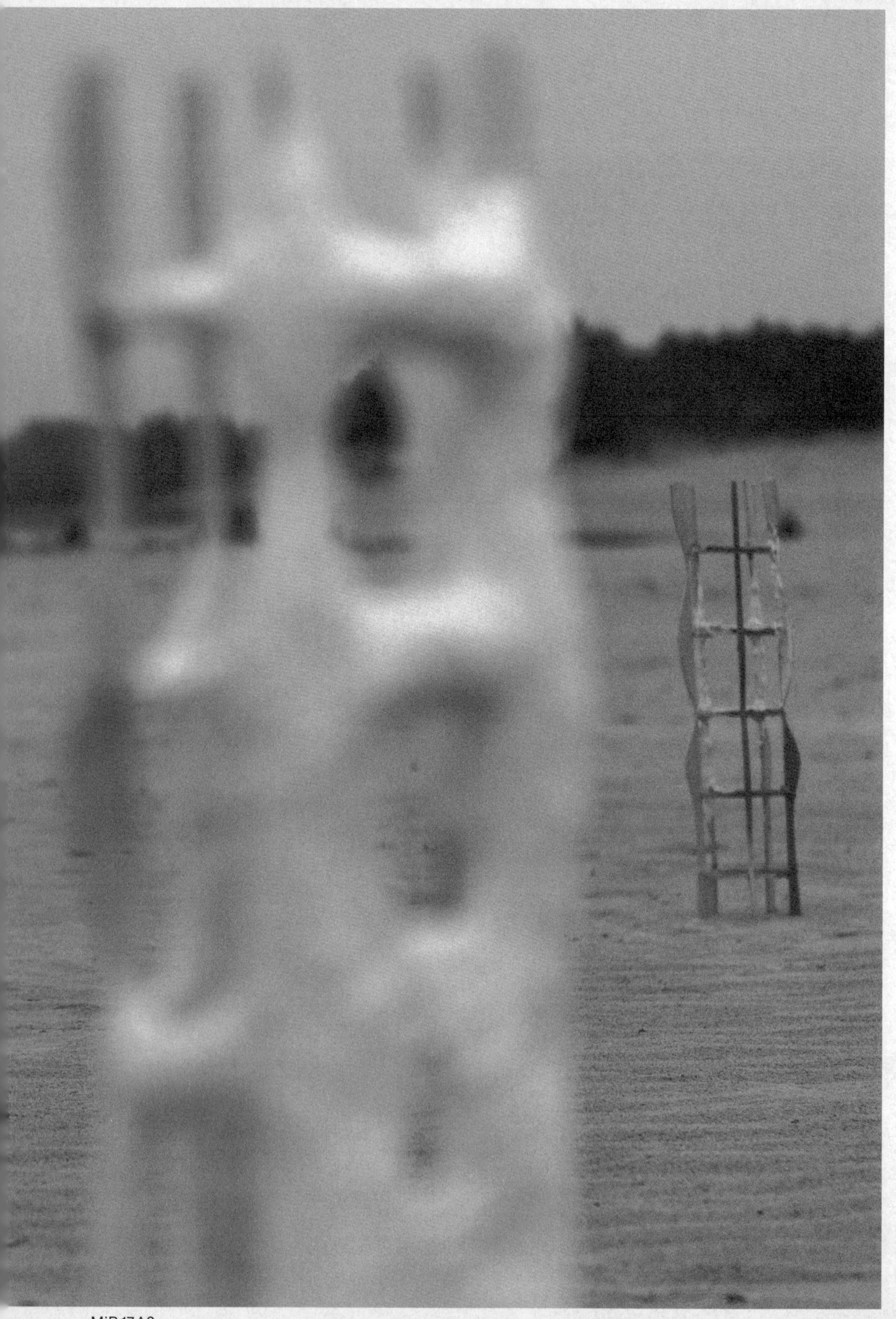

MiB.17.A2

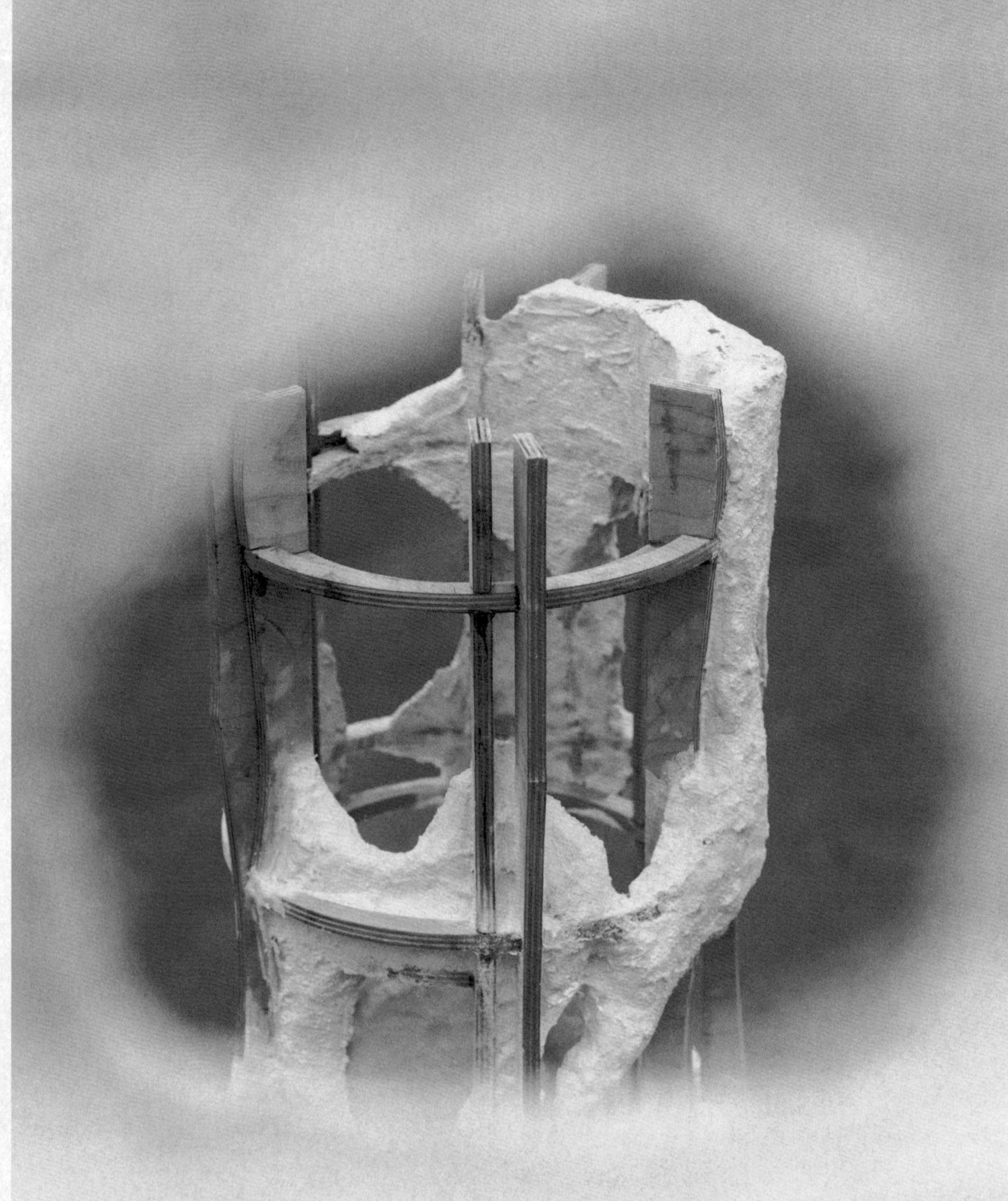

Dagmar Bosma

Dagmar Bosma

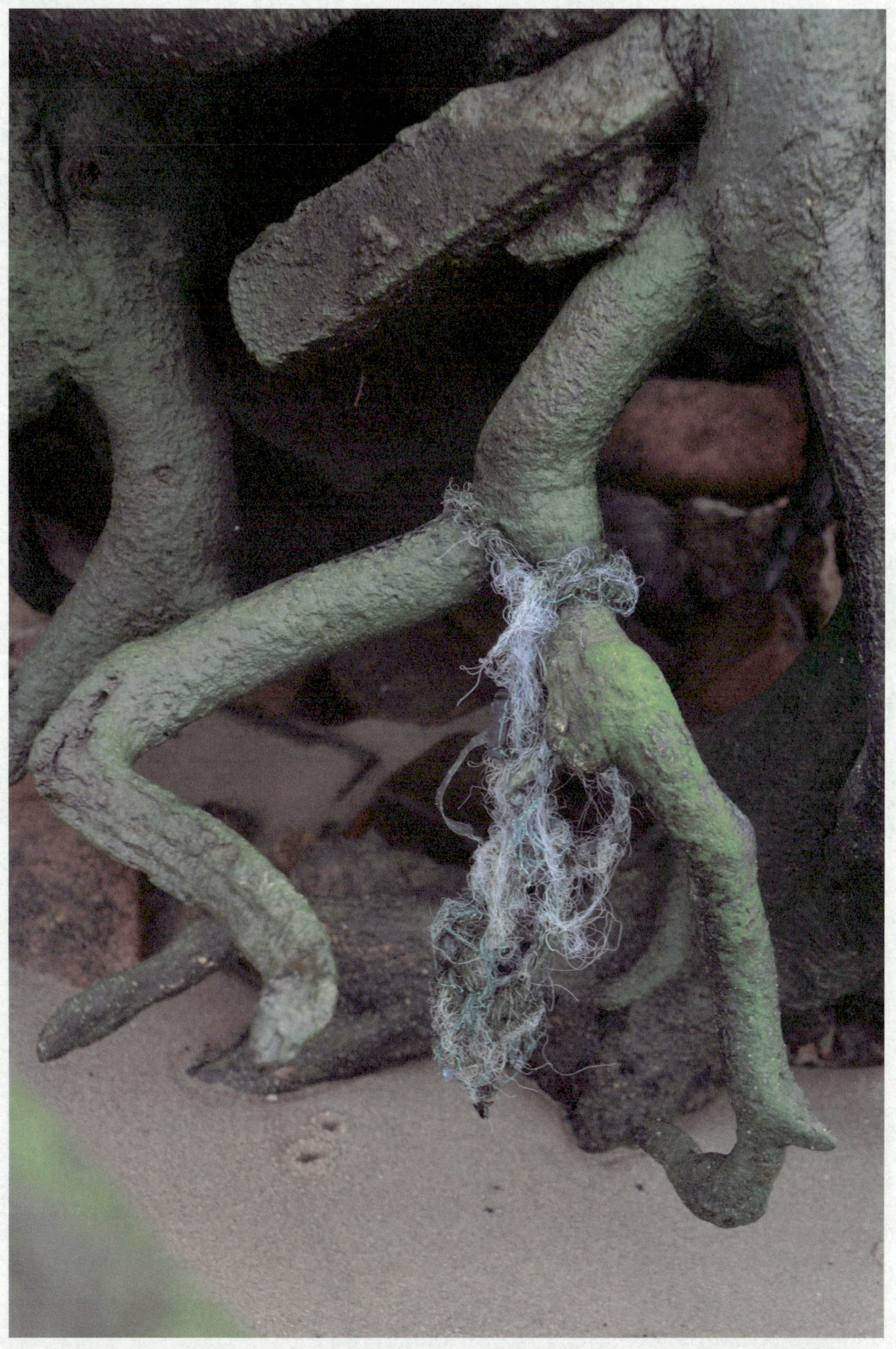

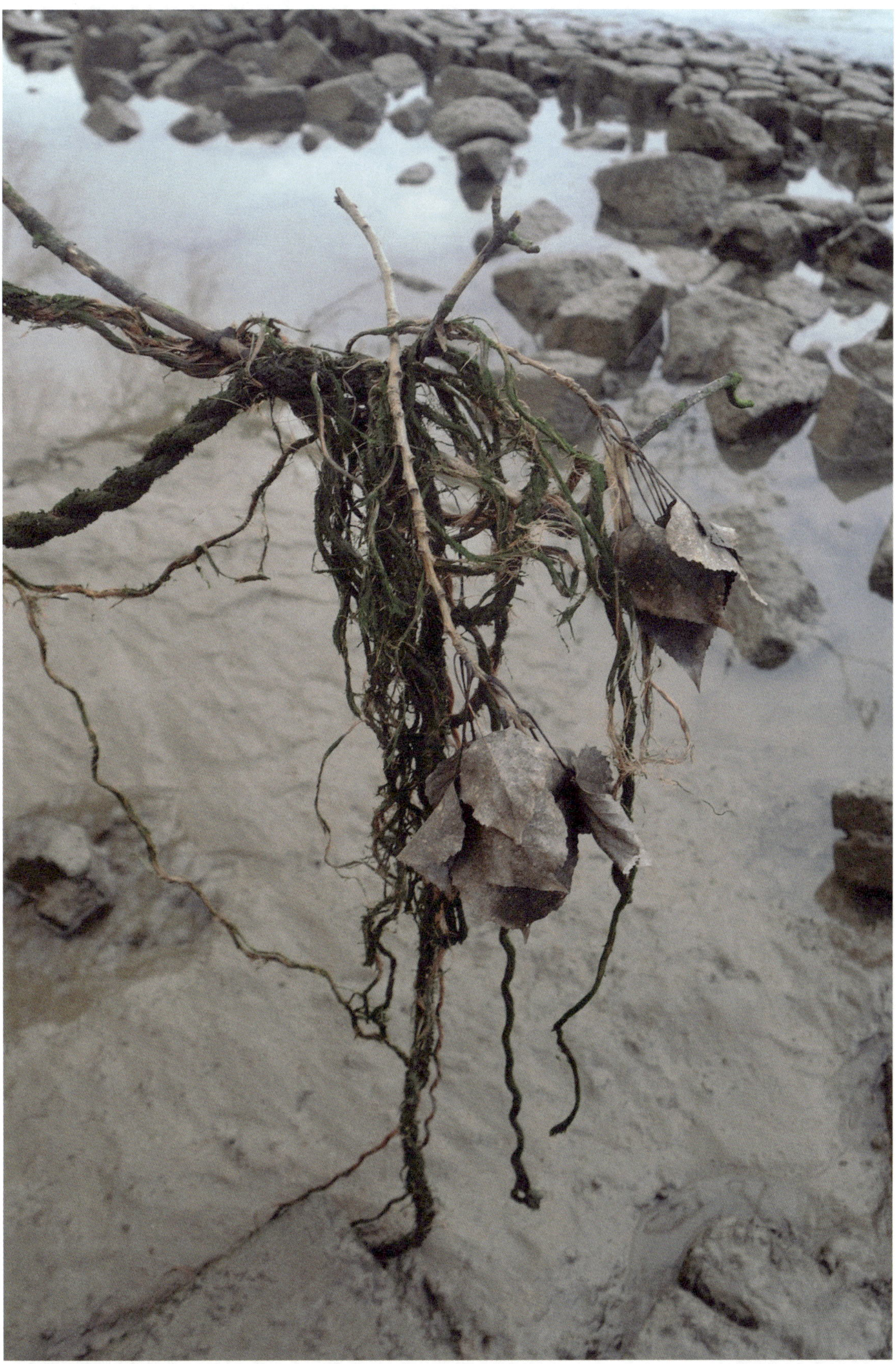

DB.02

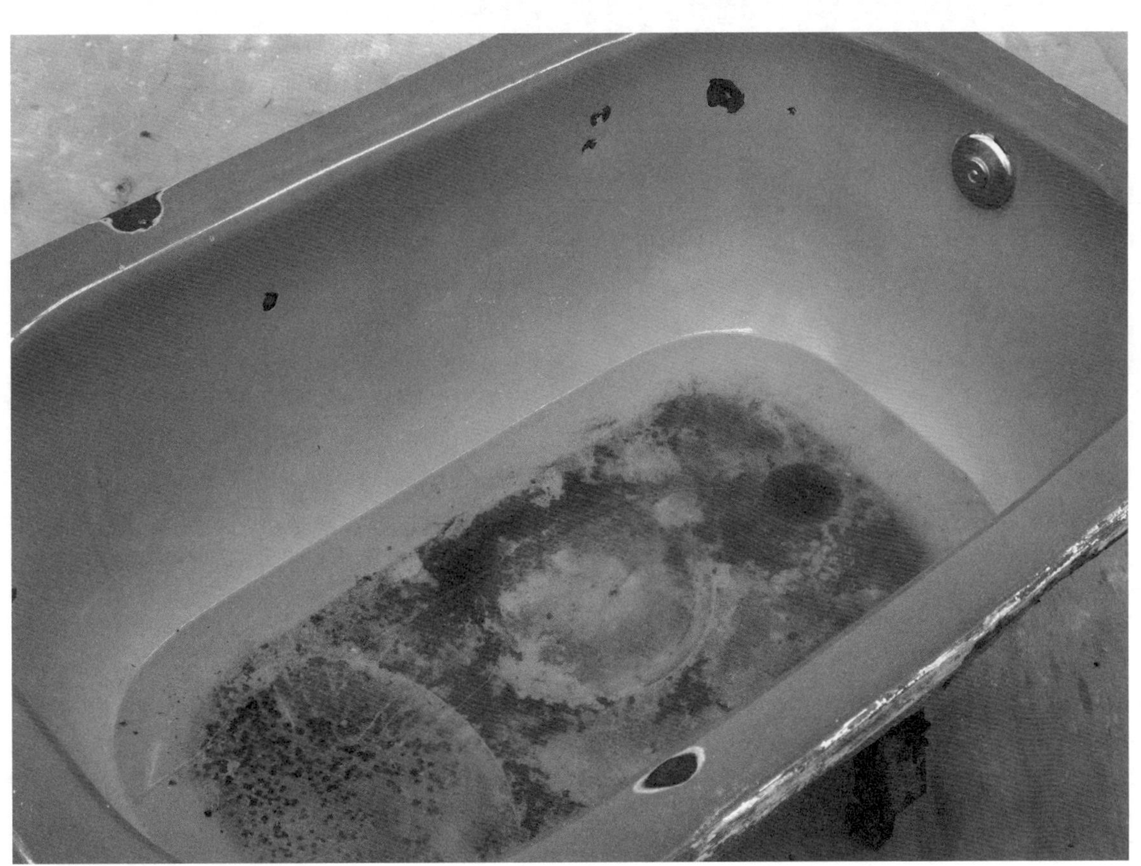

DB.03

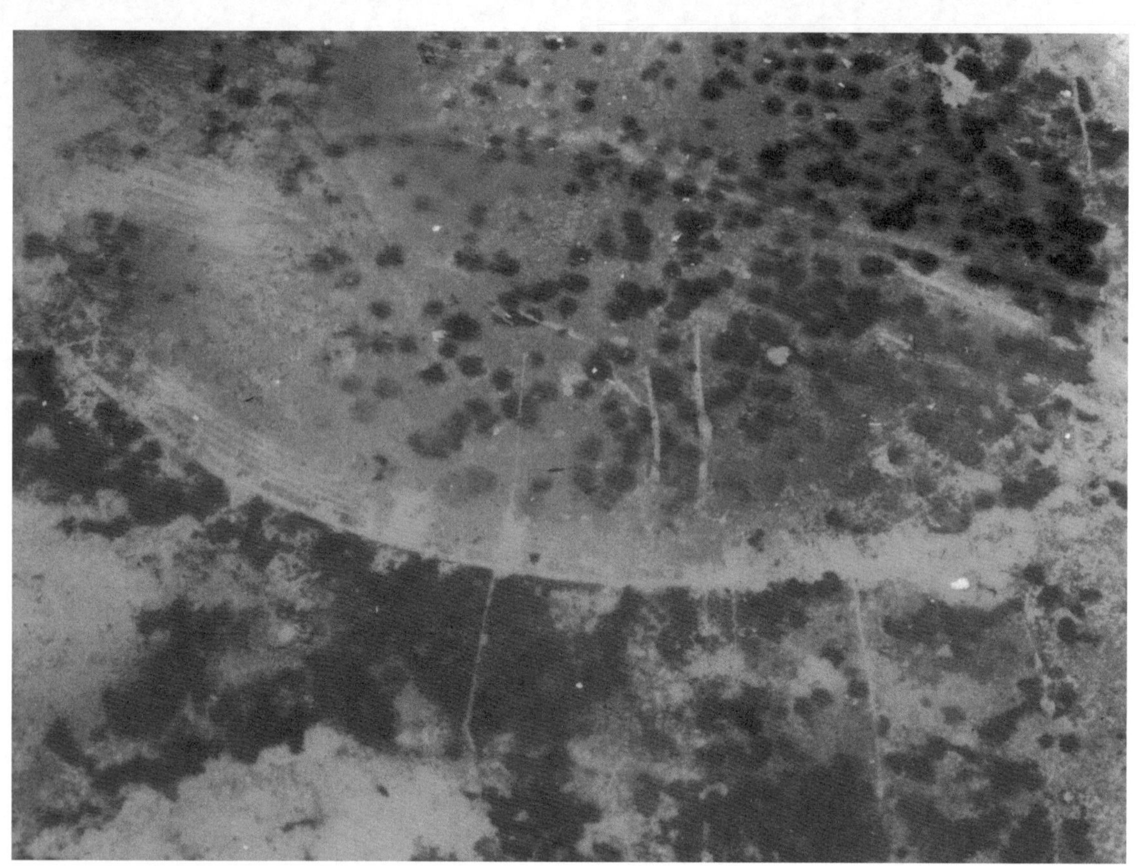

DB.04

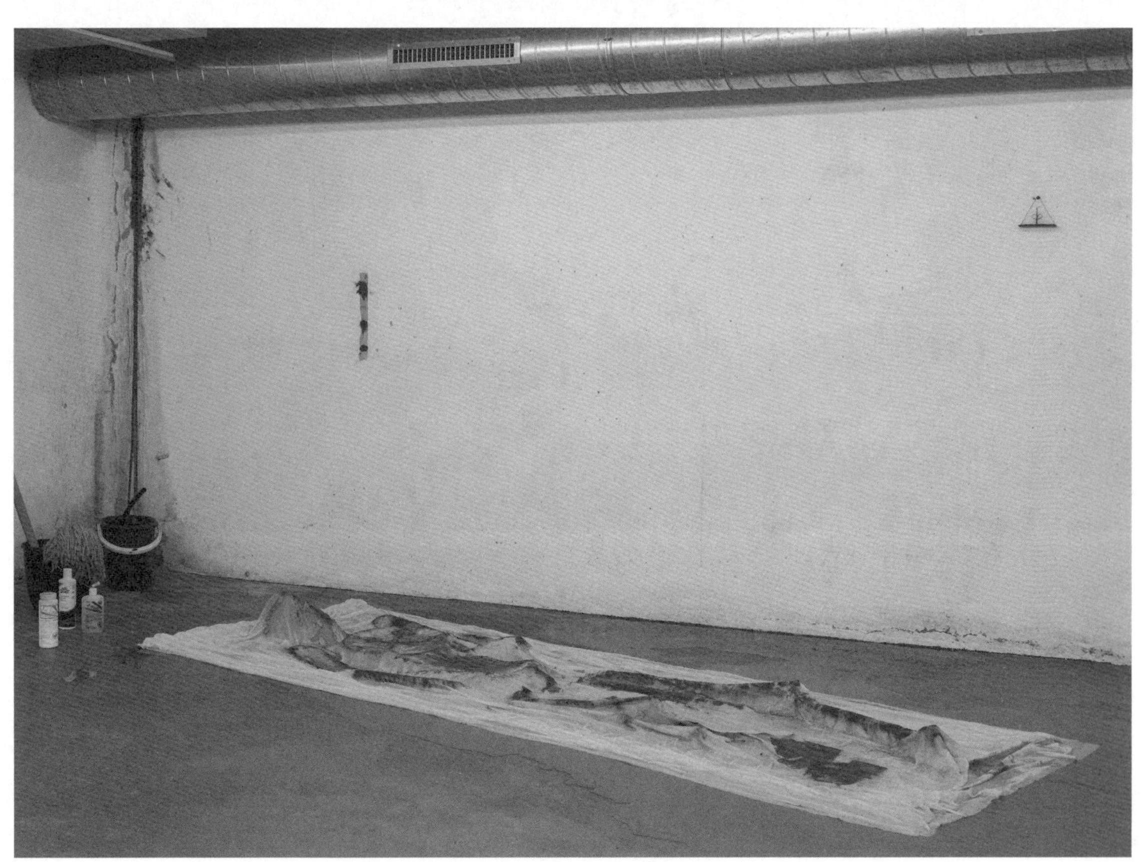

DB.05

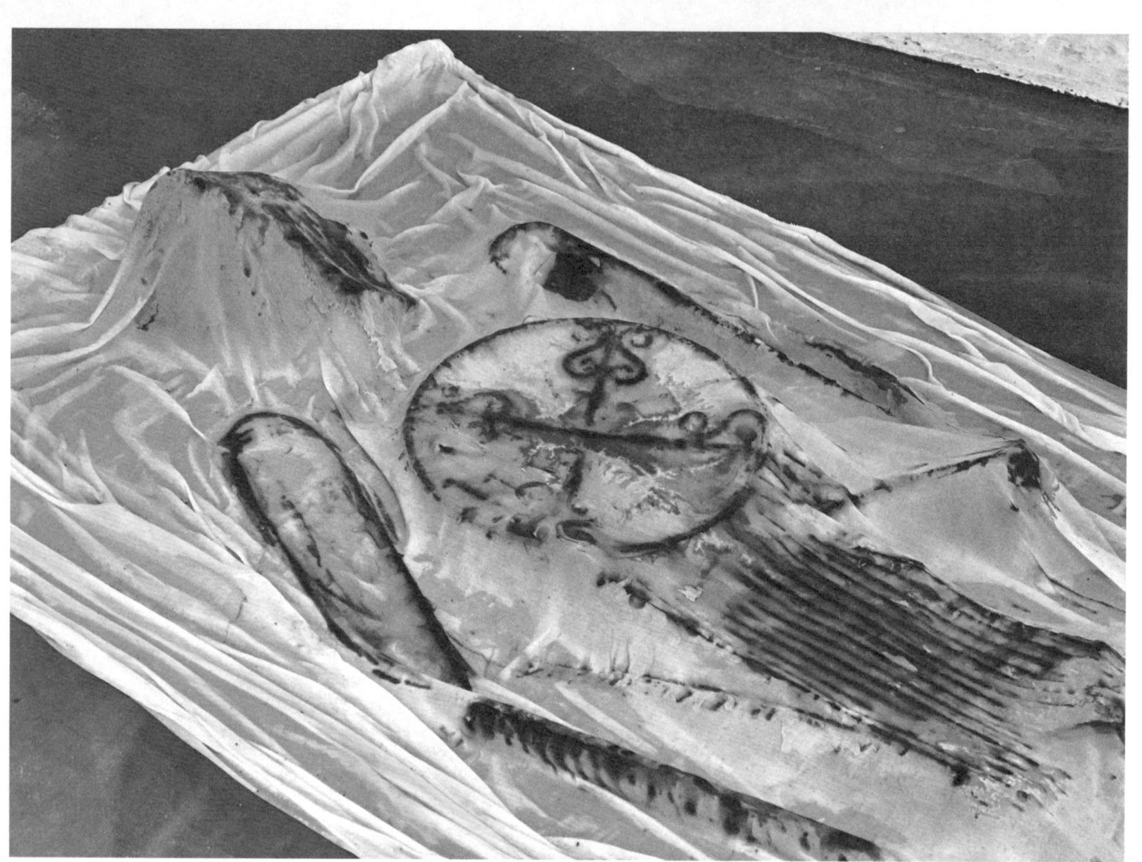

DB.06

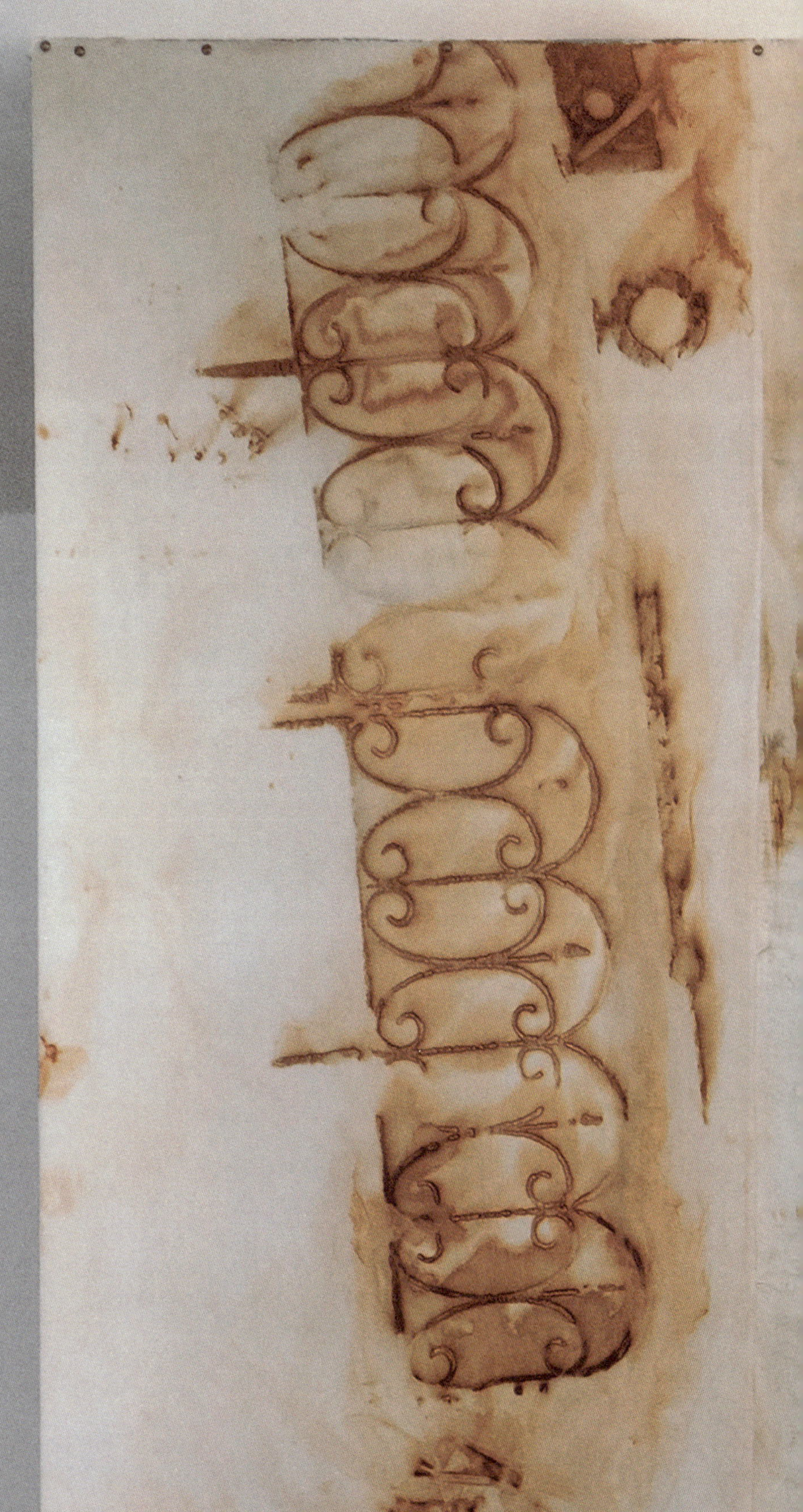

DB.07.A1

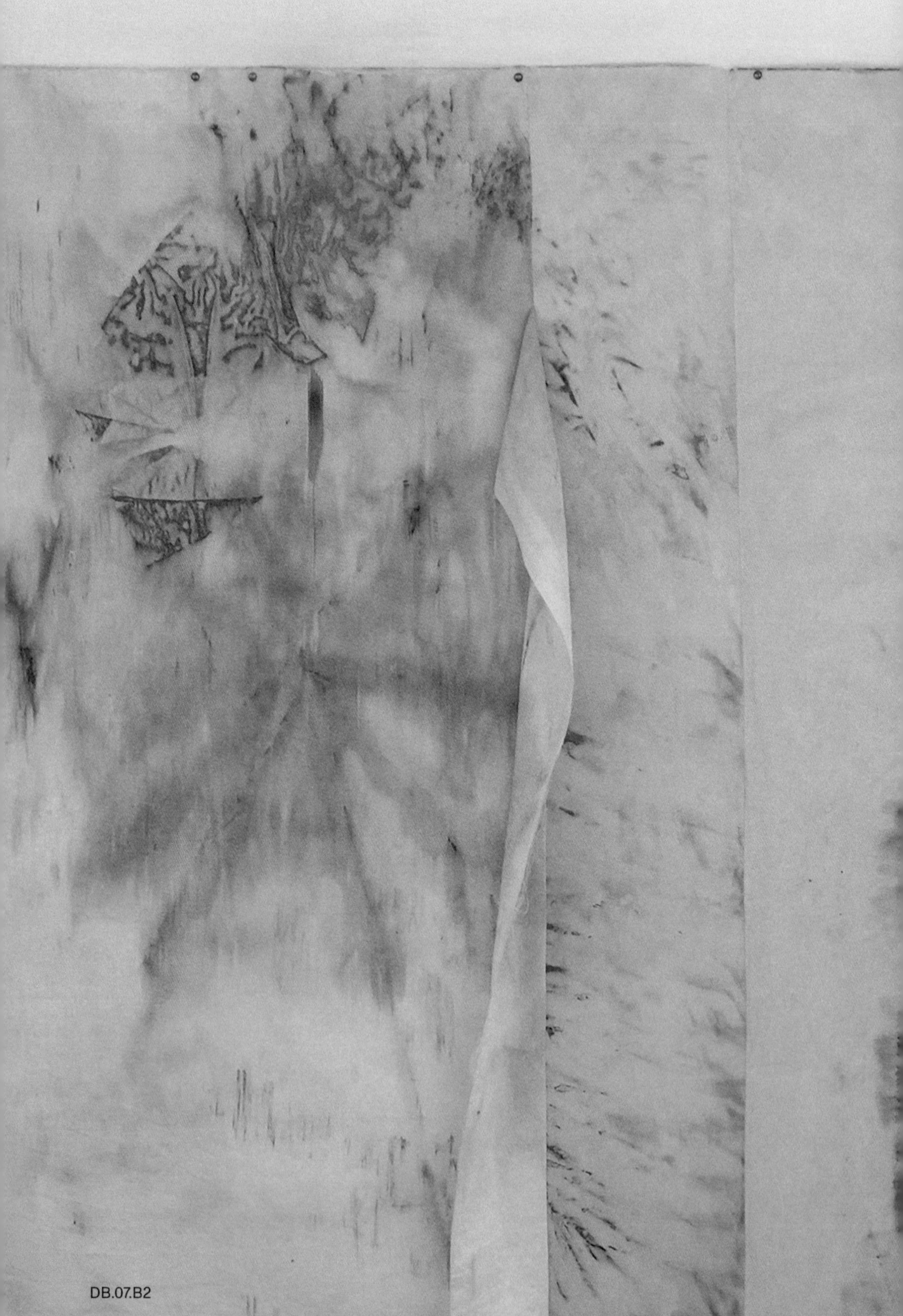

DB.07.B2

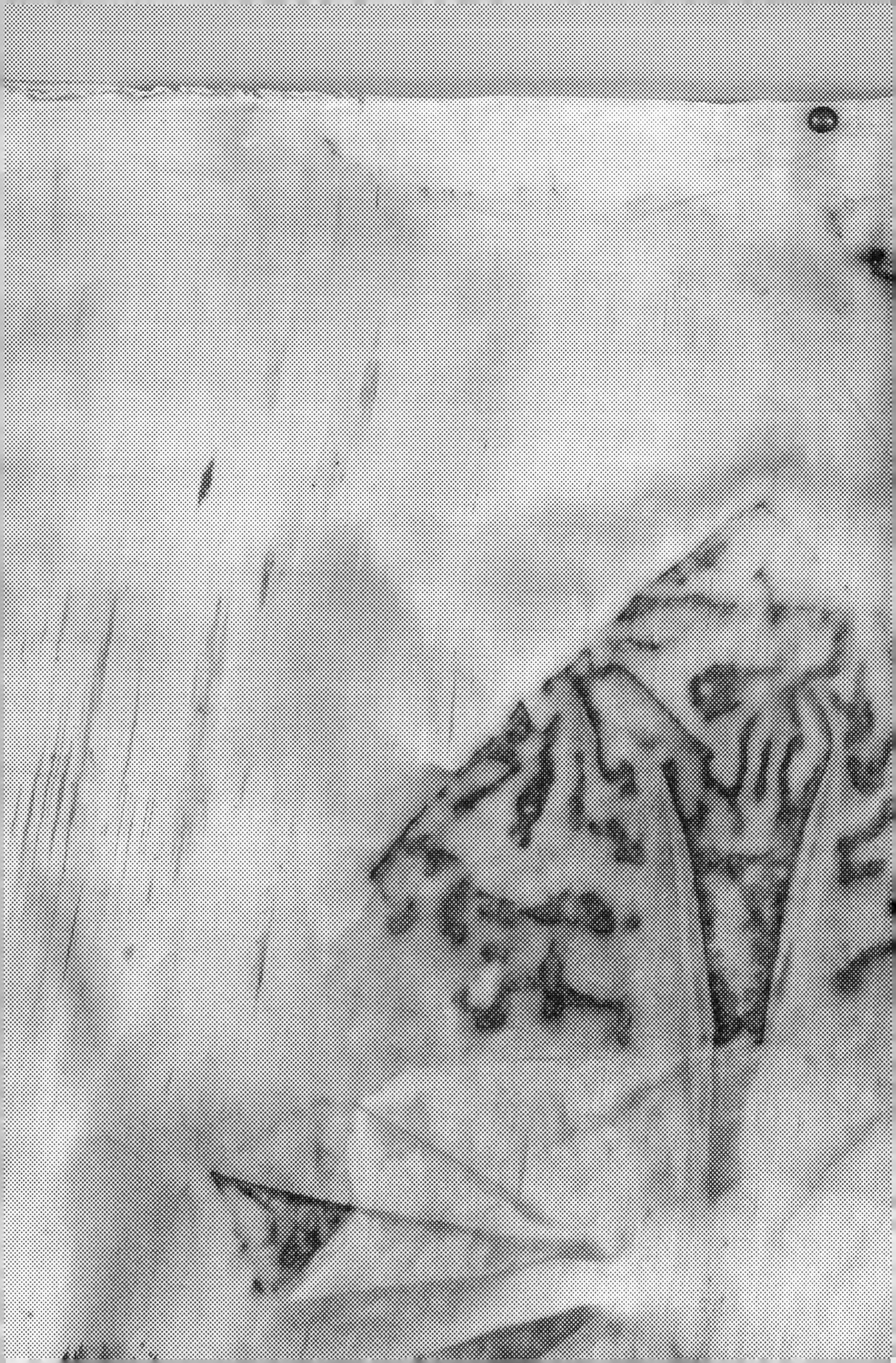

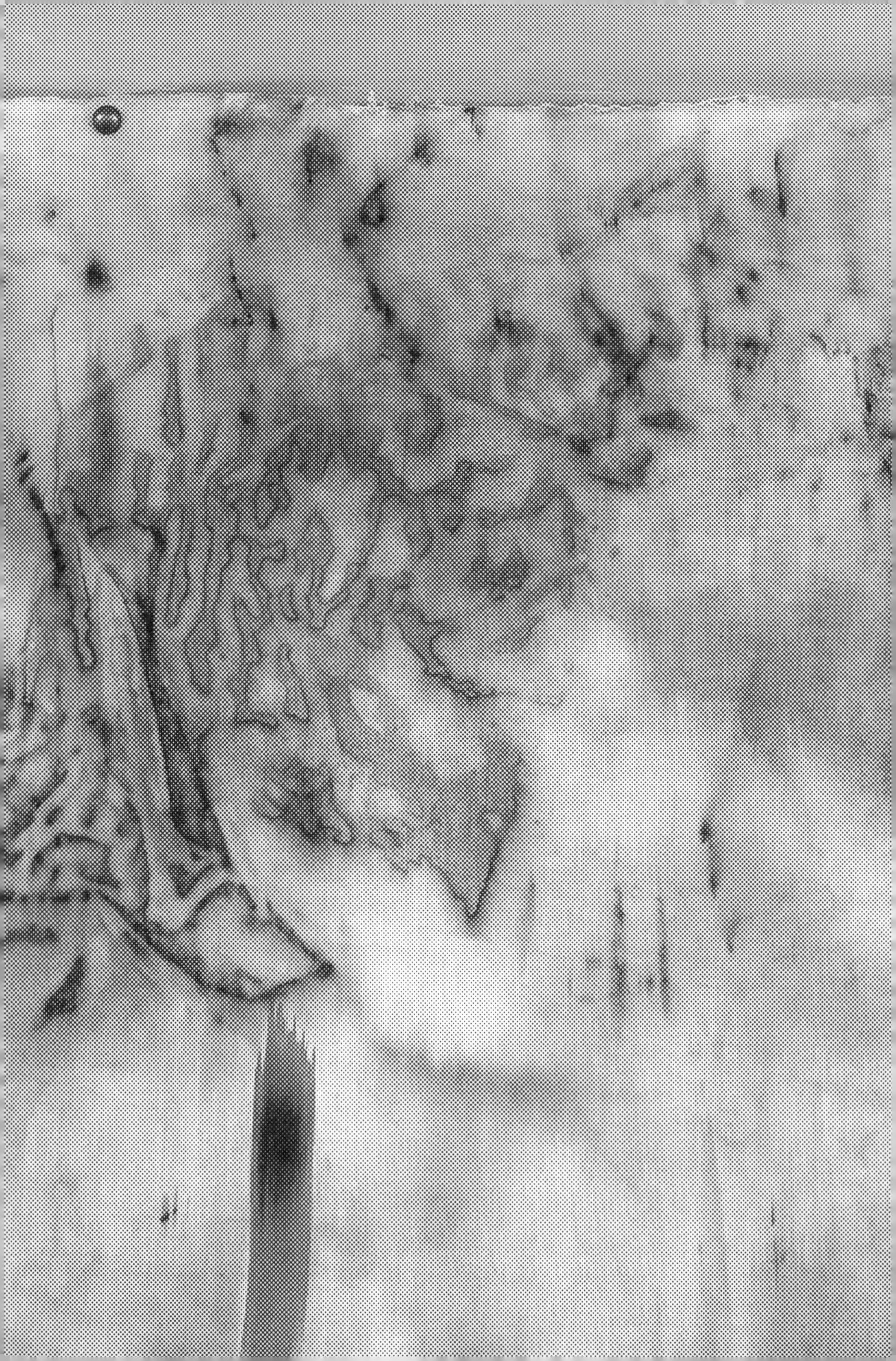

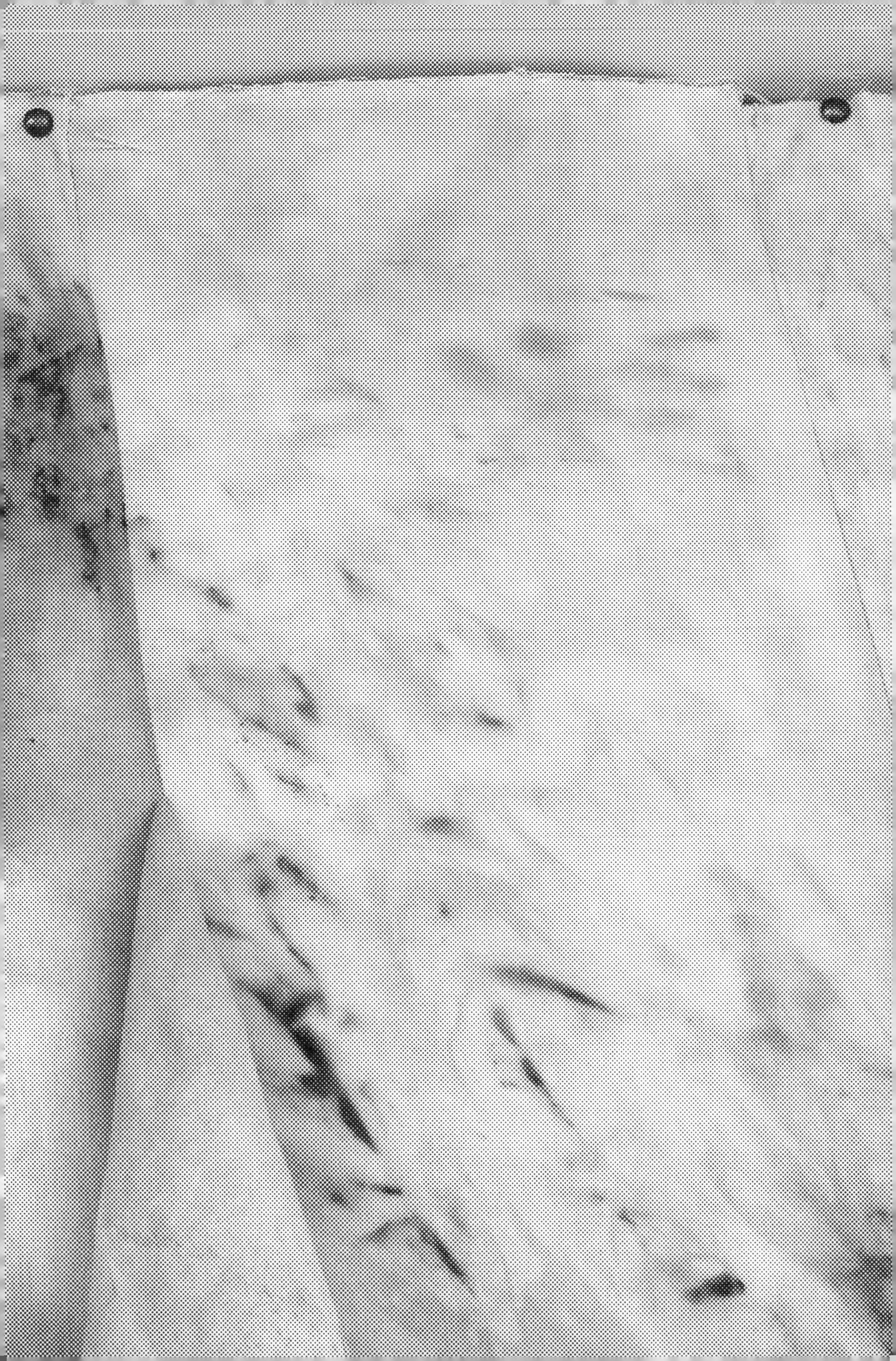

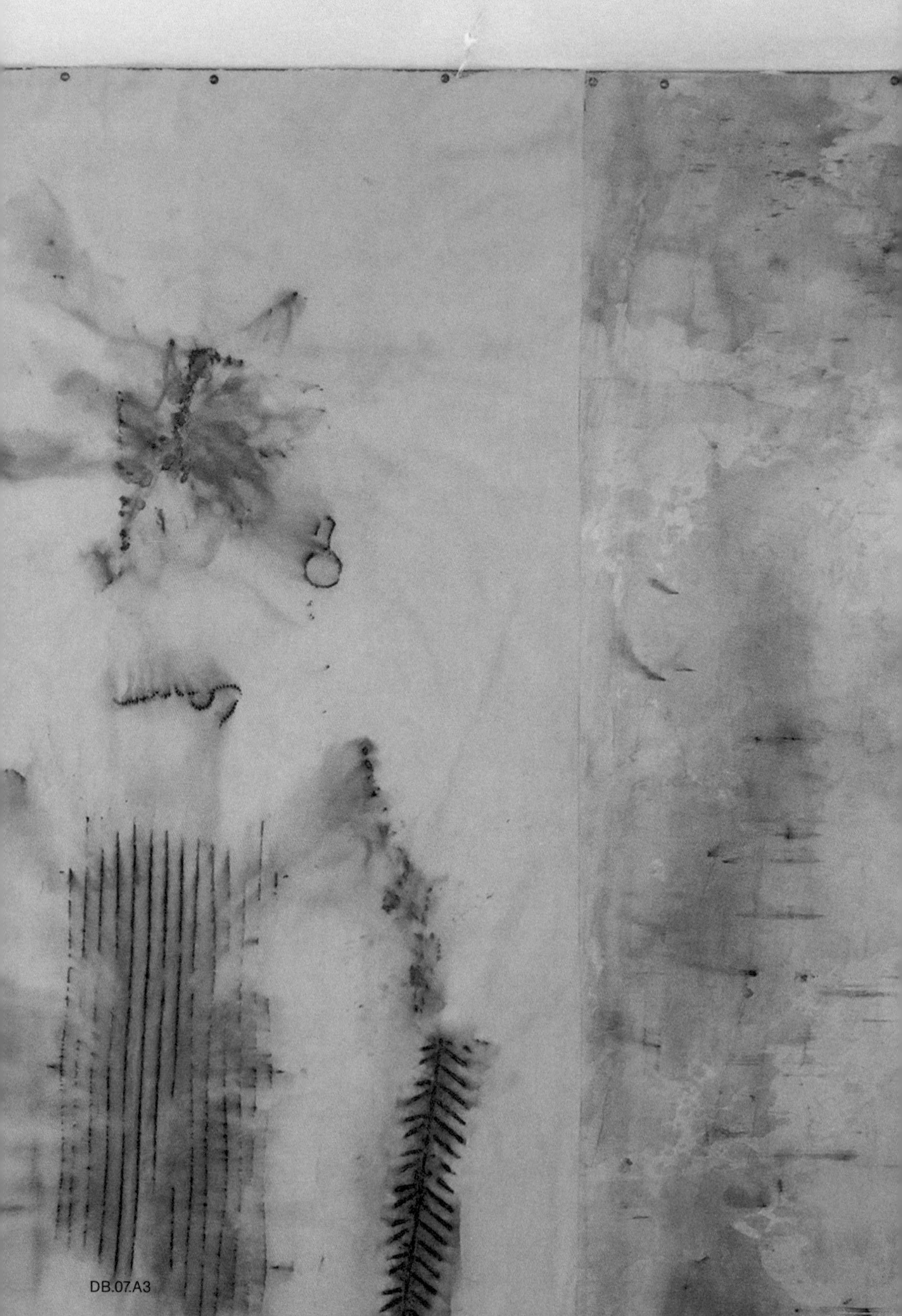

DB.07.A3

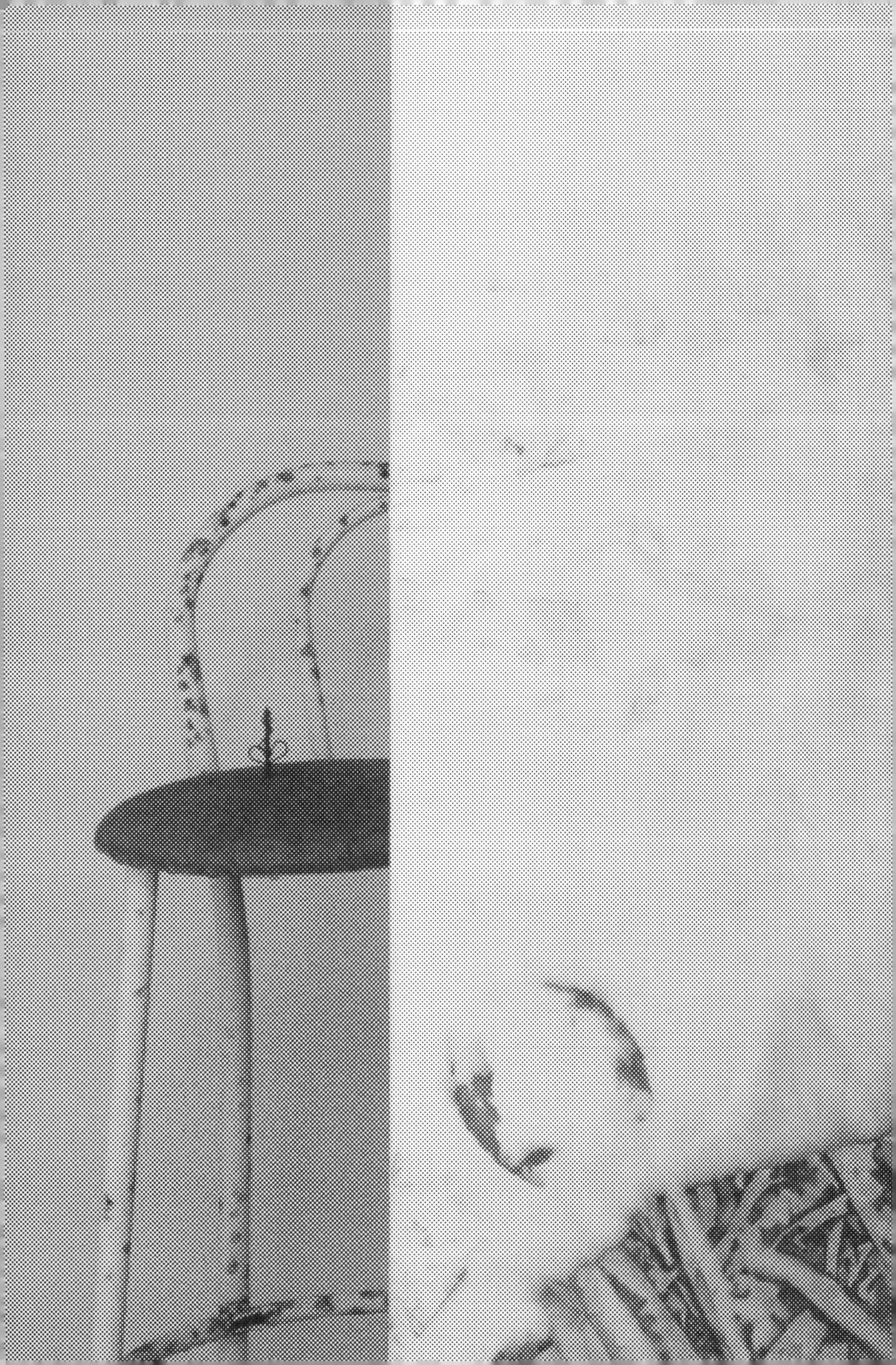

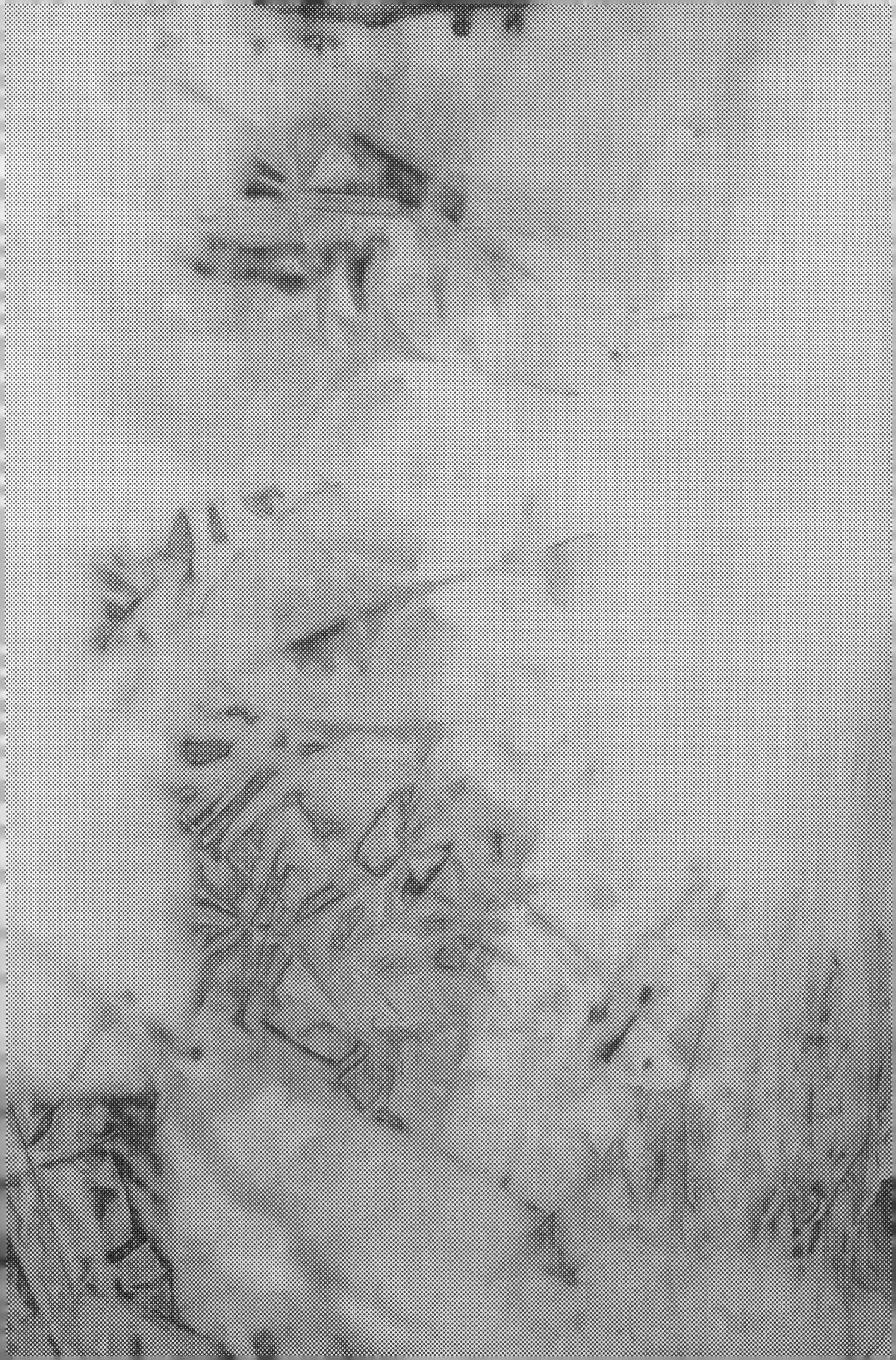

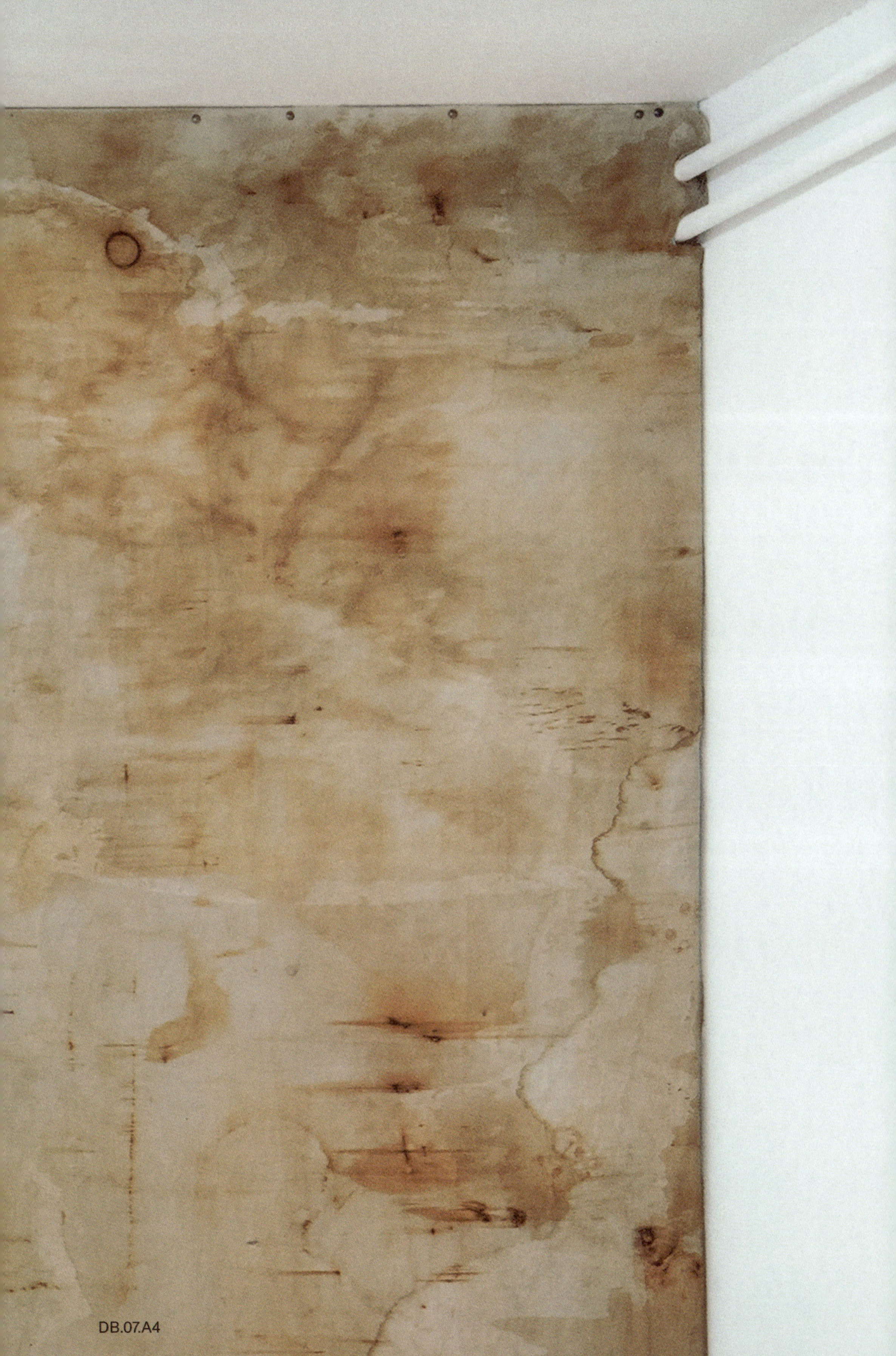

DB.07.A4

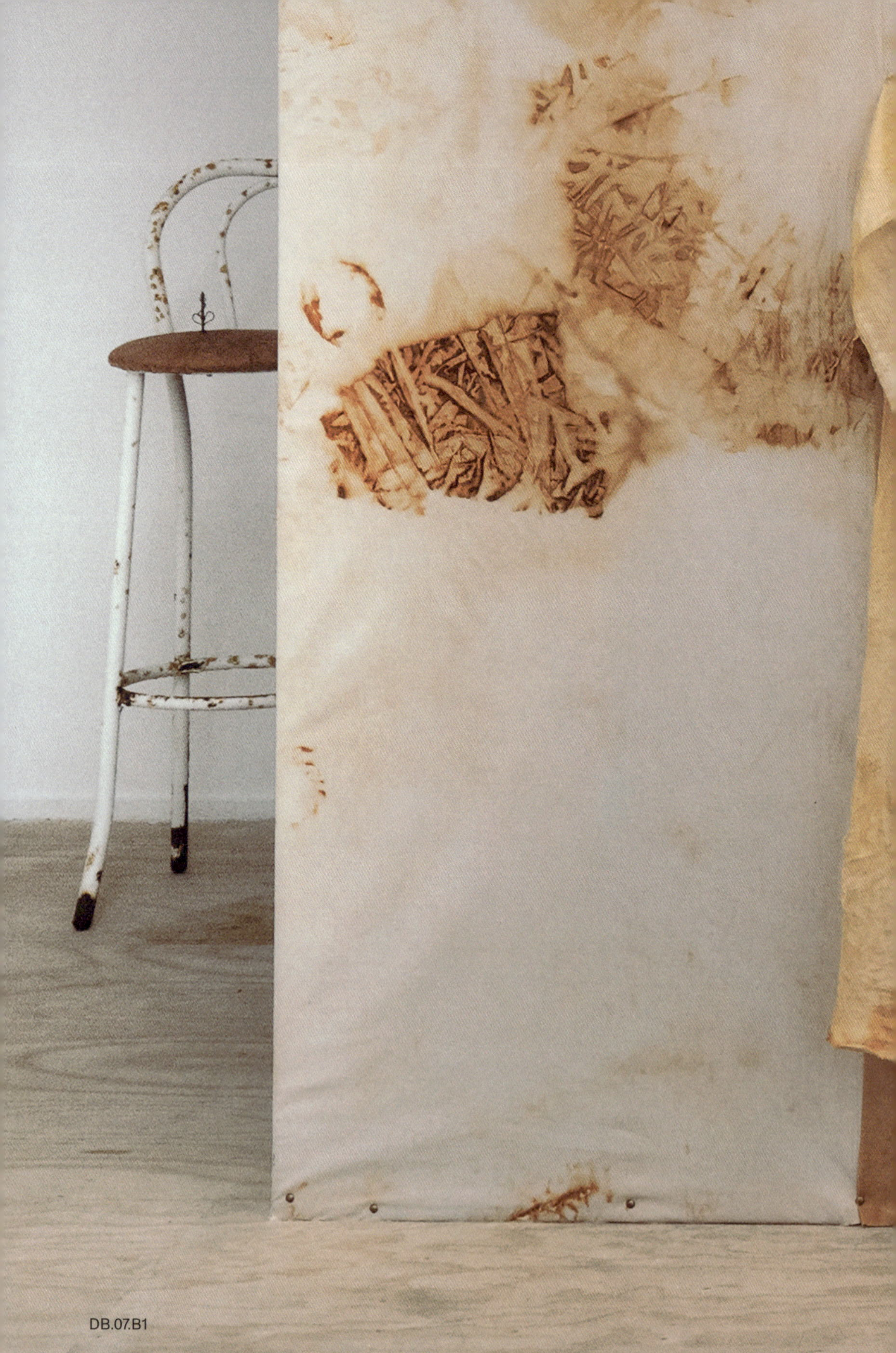
DB.07.B1

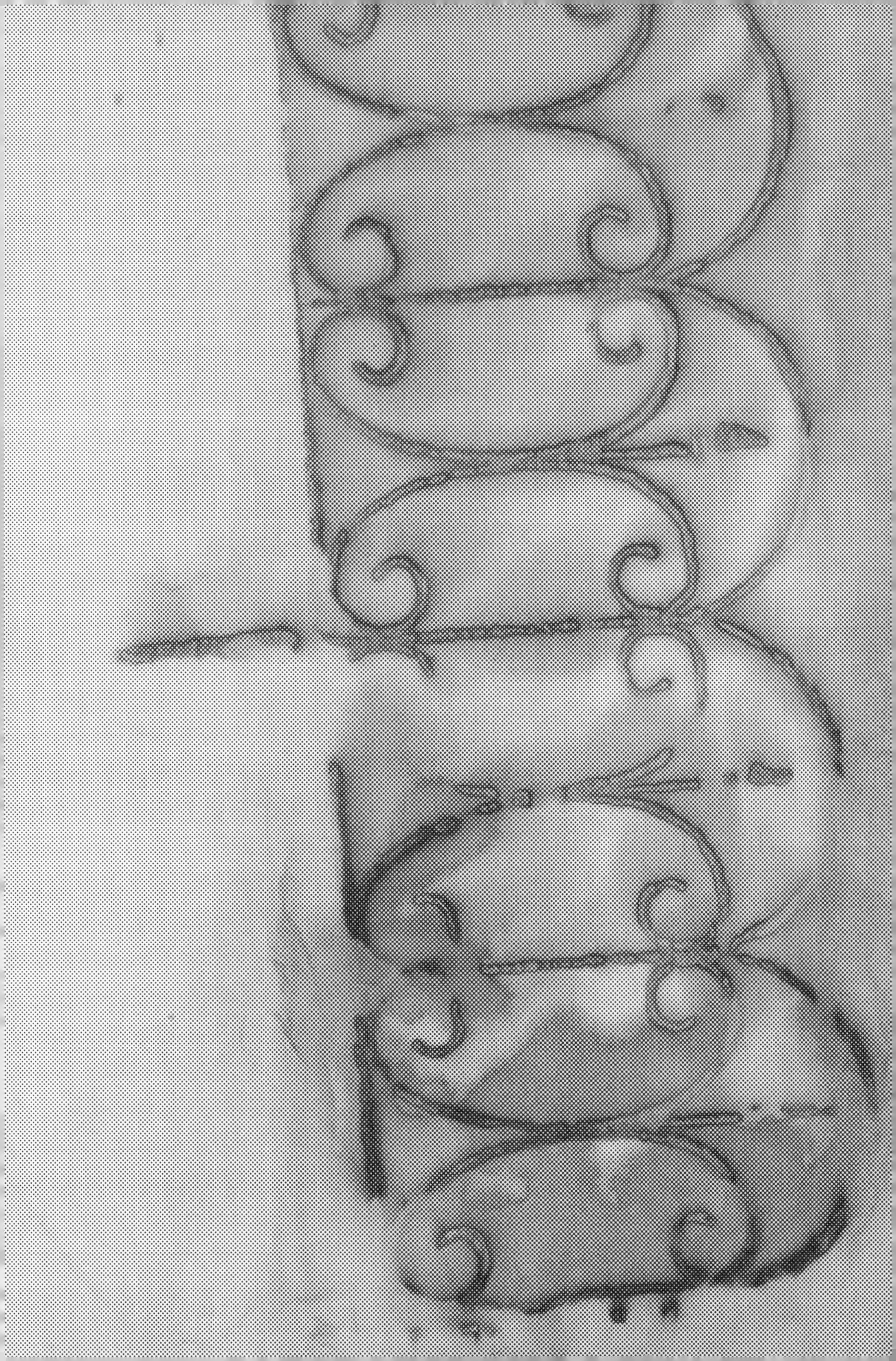

DB.07.B2

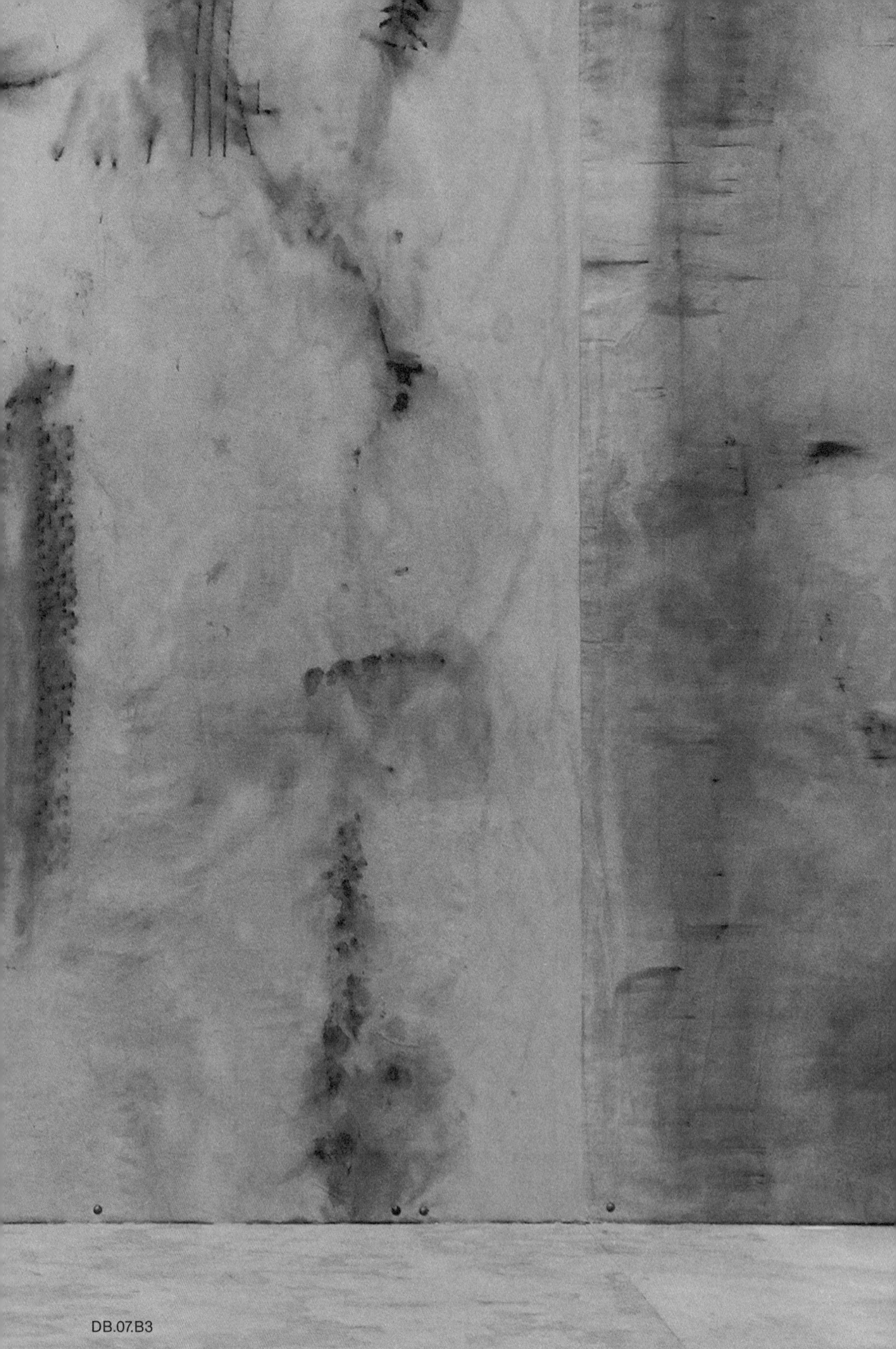

DB.07.B3

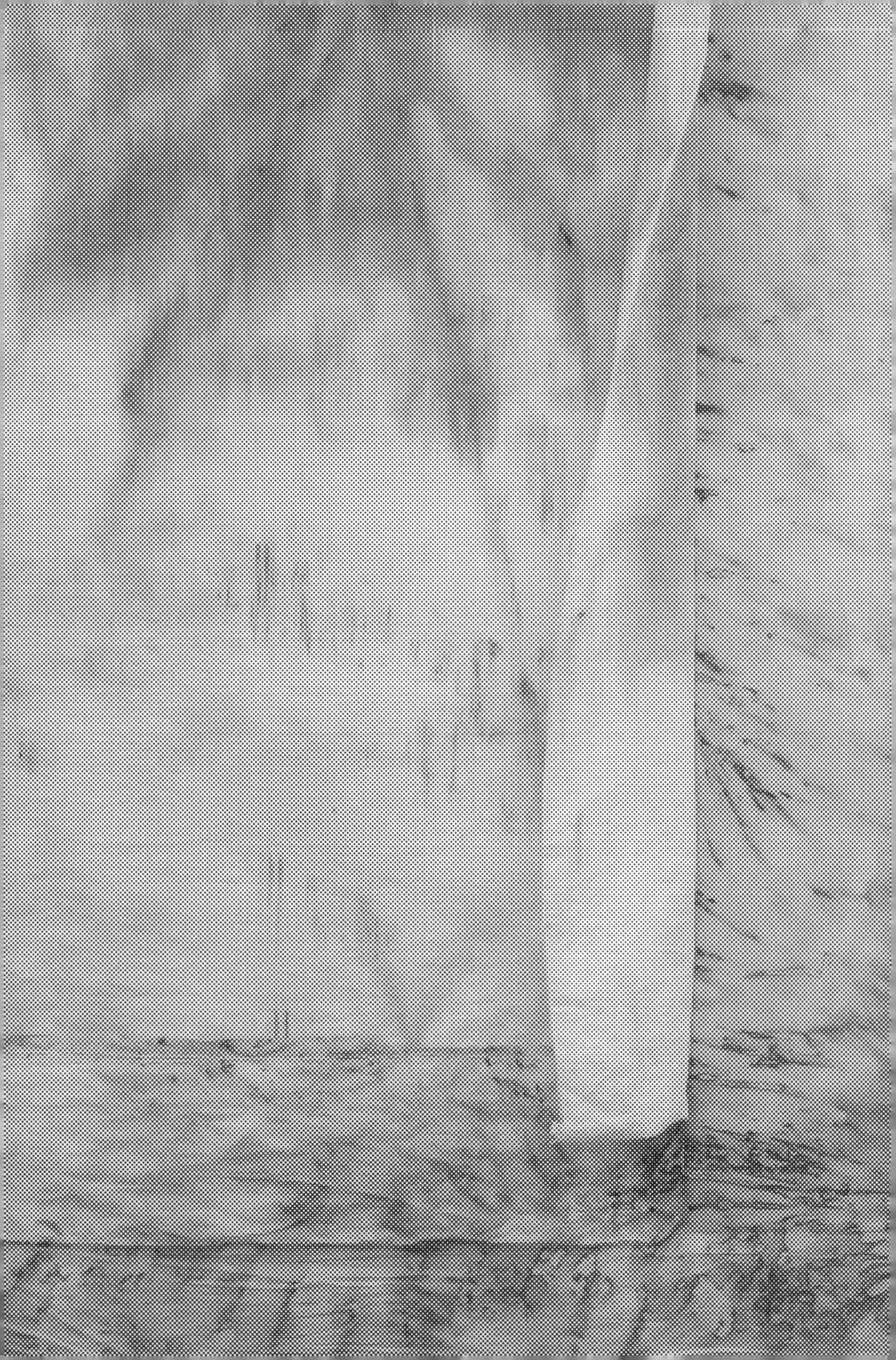

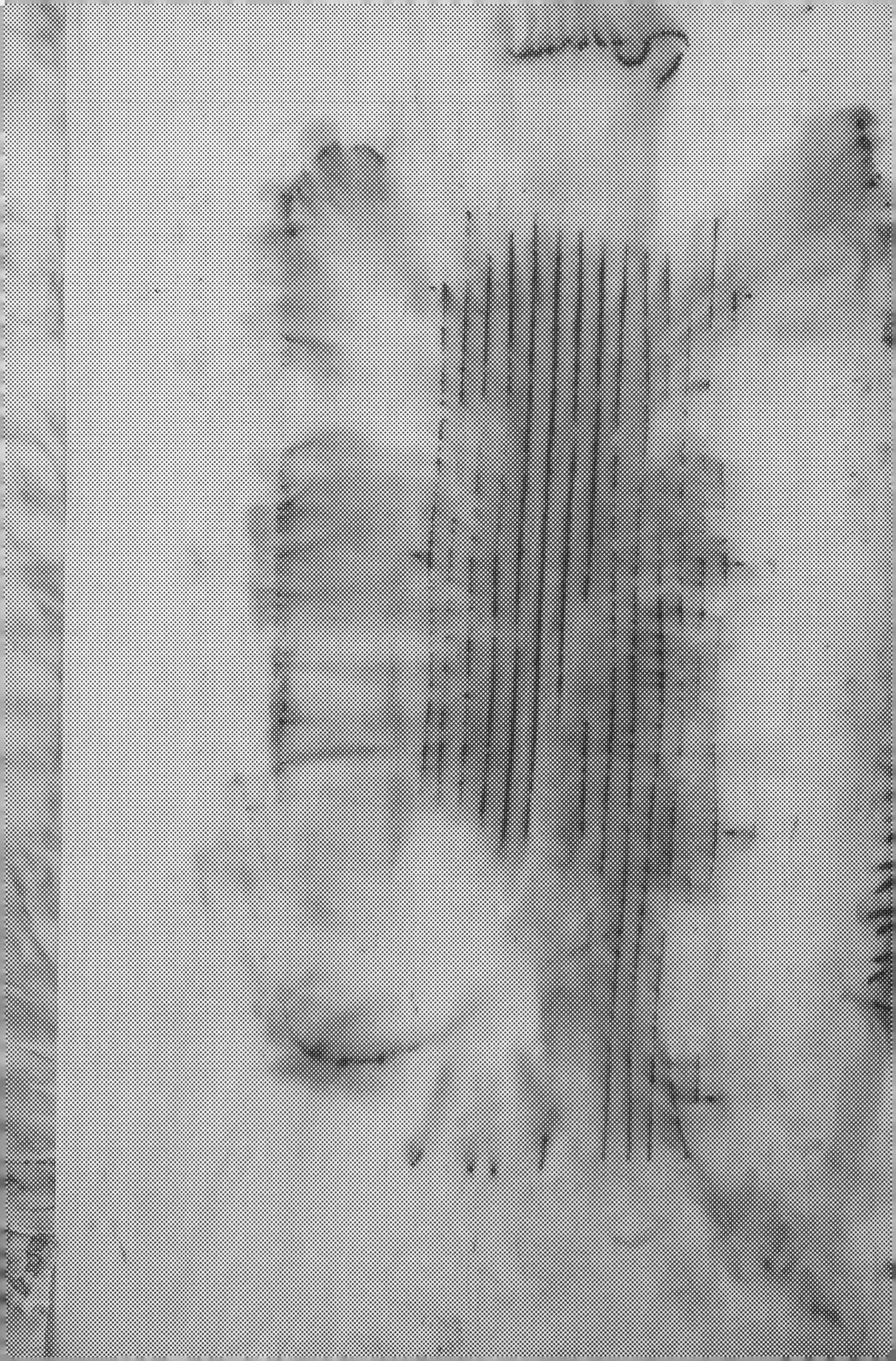

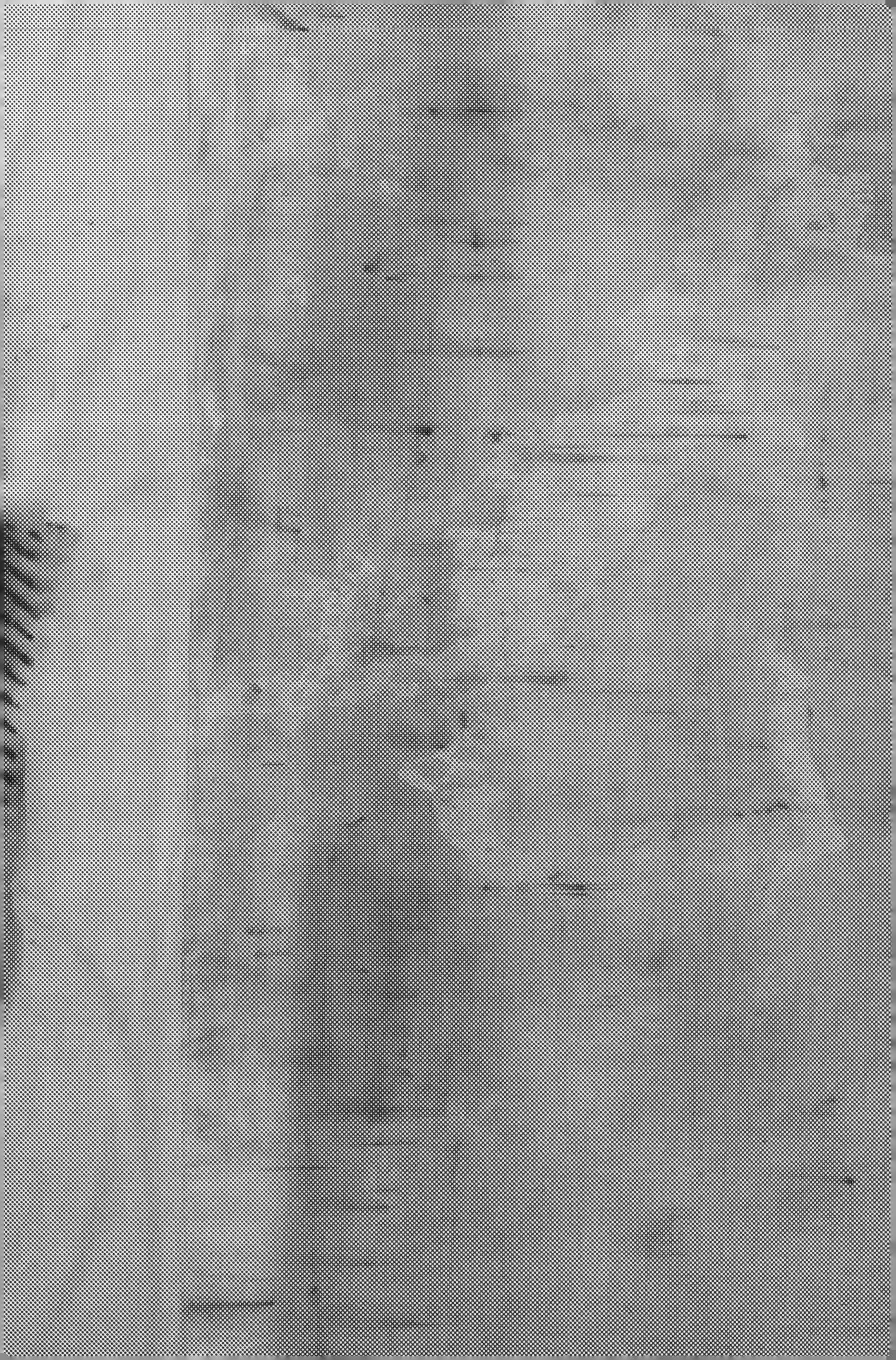

DB.07.B4

Lara Almarcegui

Lara Almarcegui

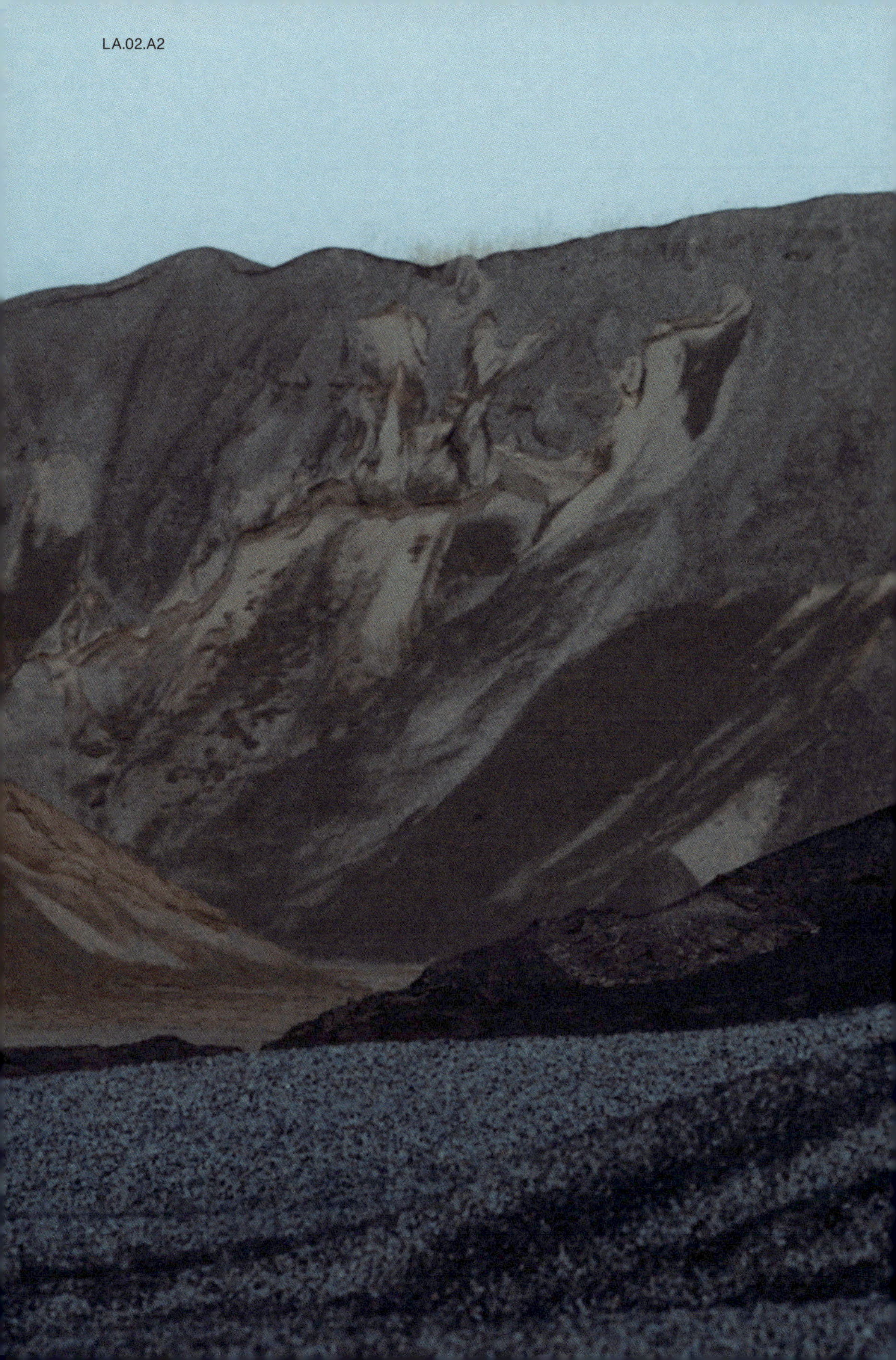

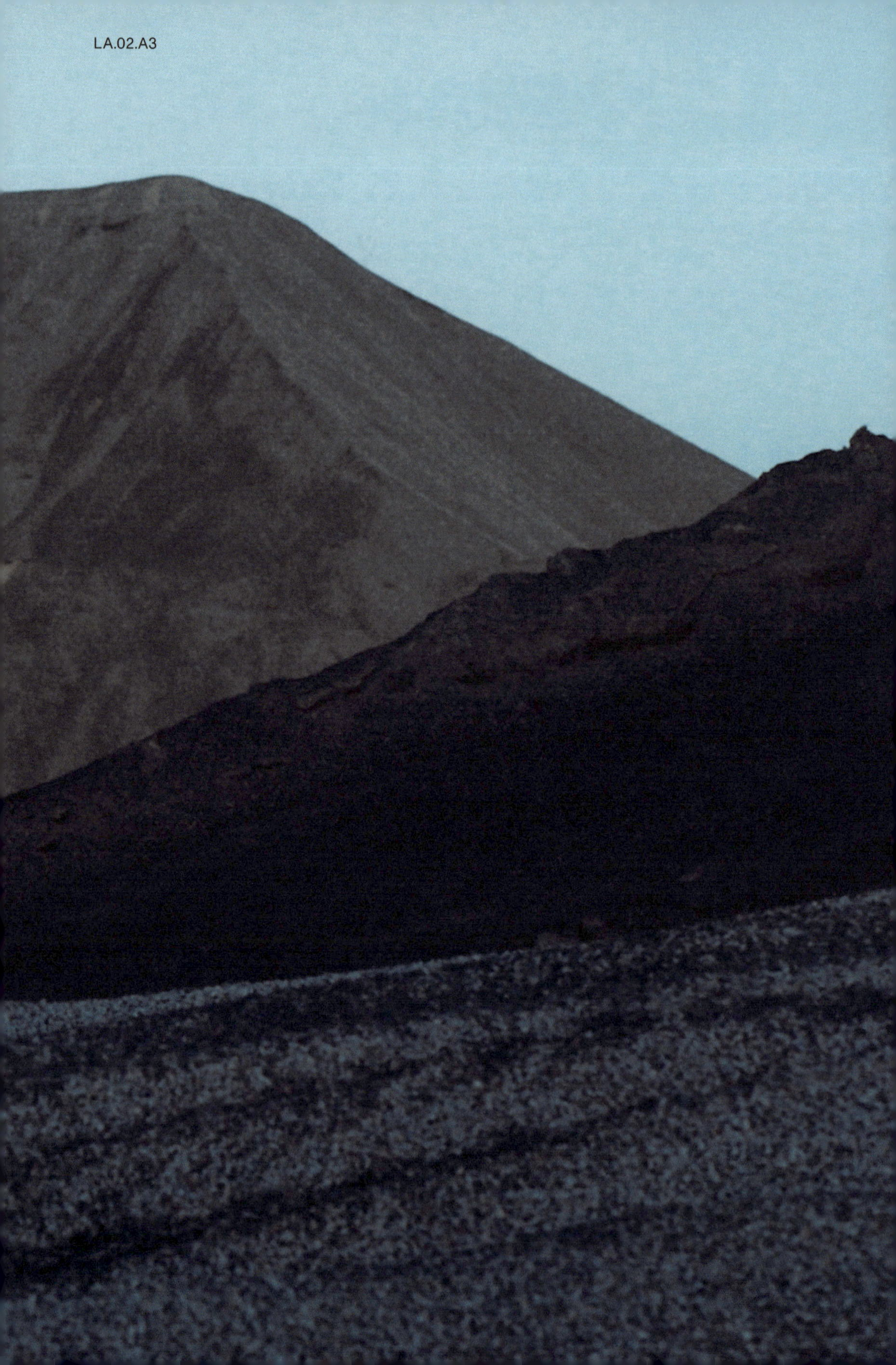
LA.02.A3

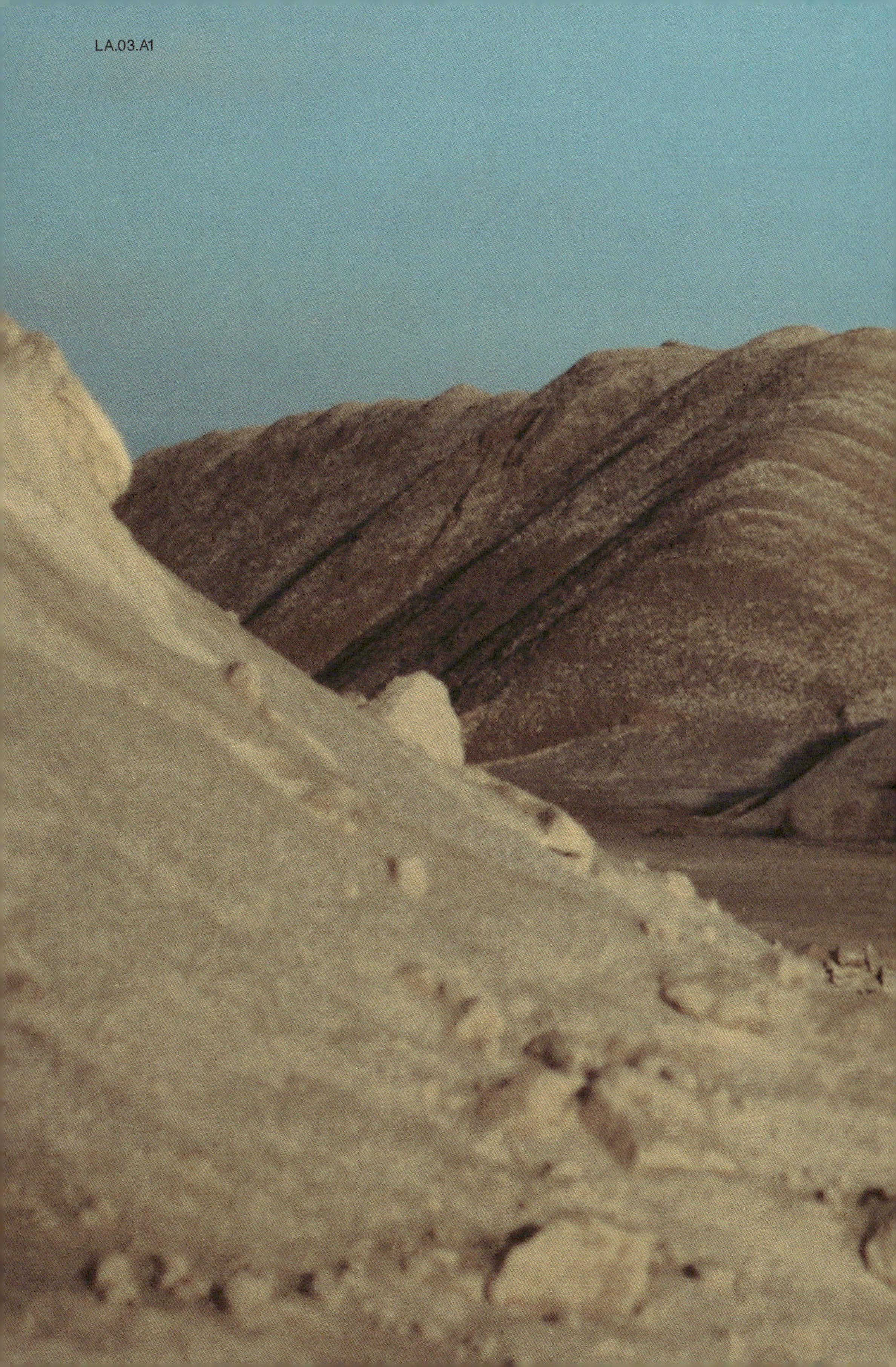

LA.03.A1

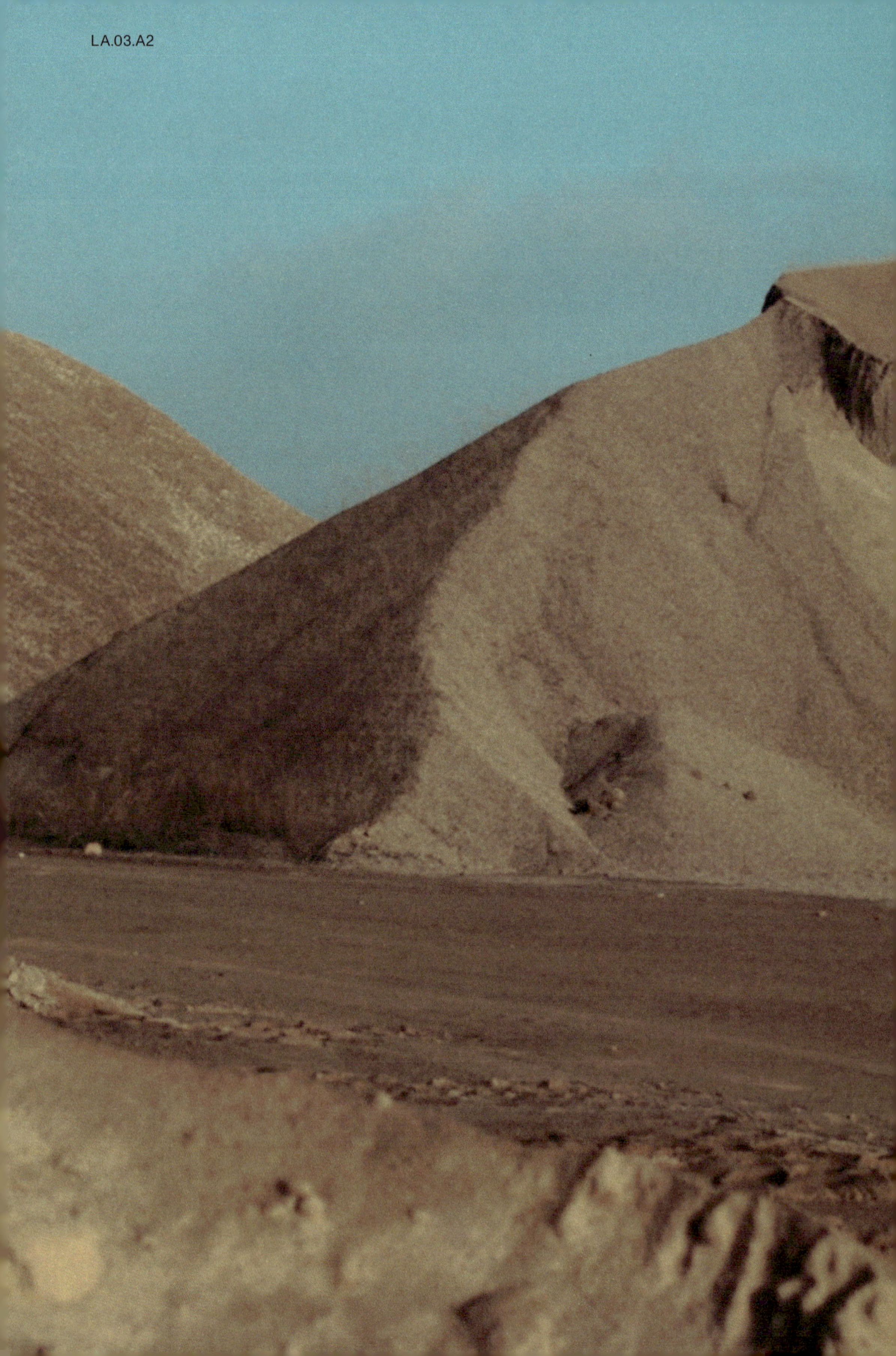
LA.03.A2

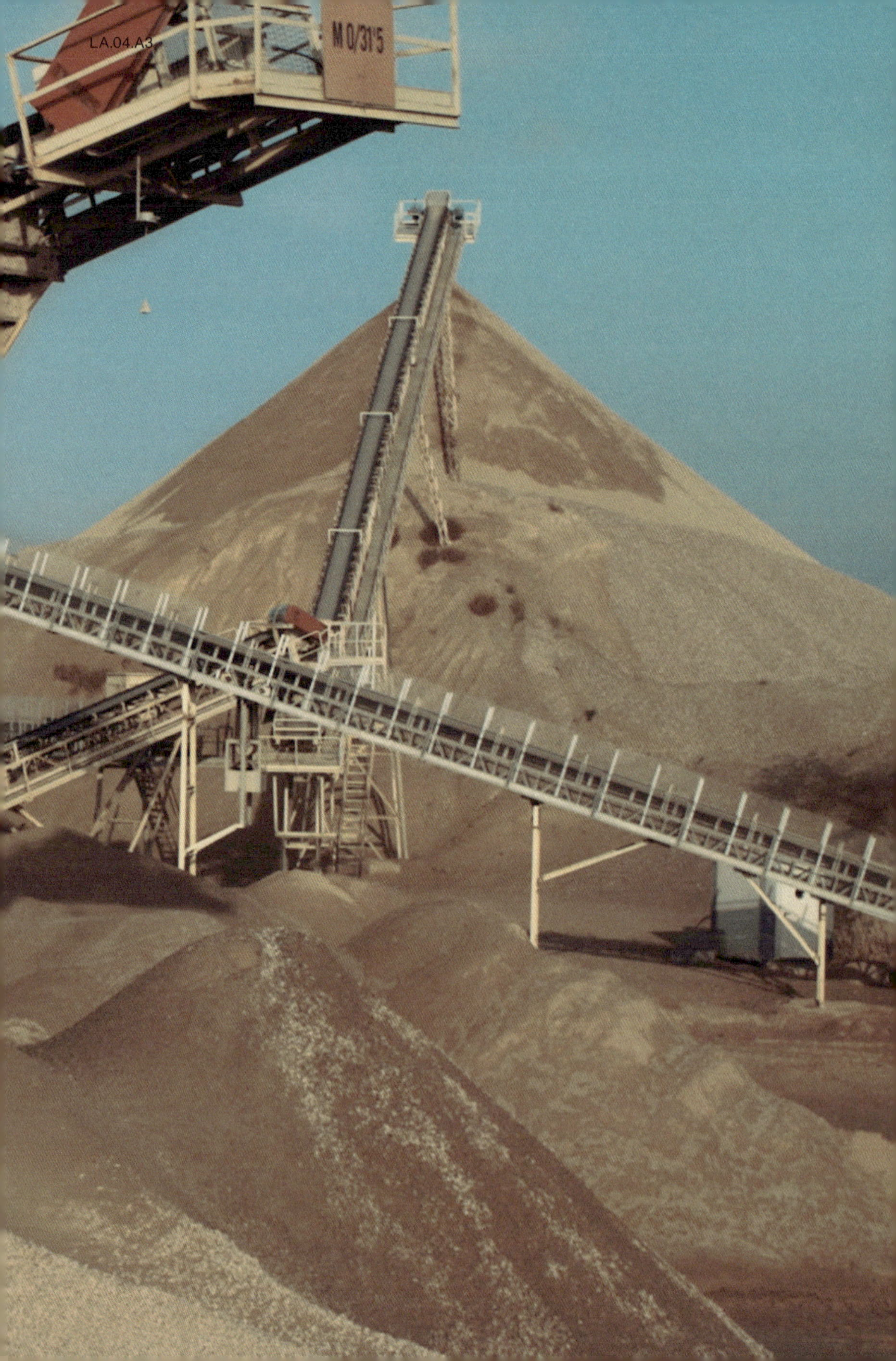

LA.04.A3
M 0/31'5

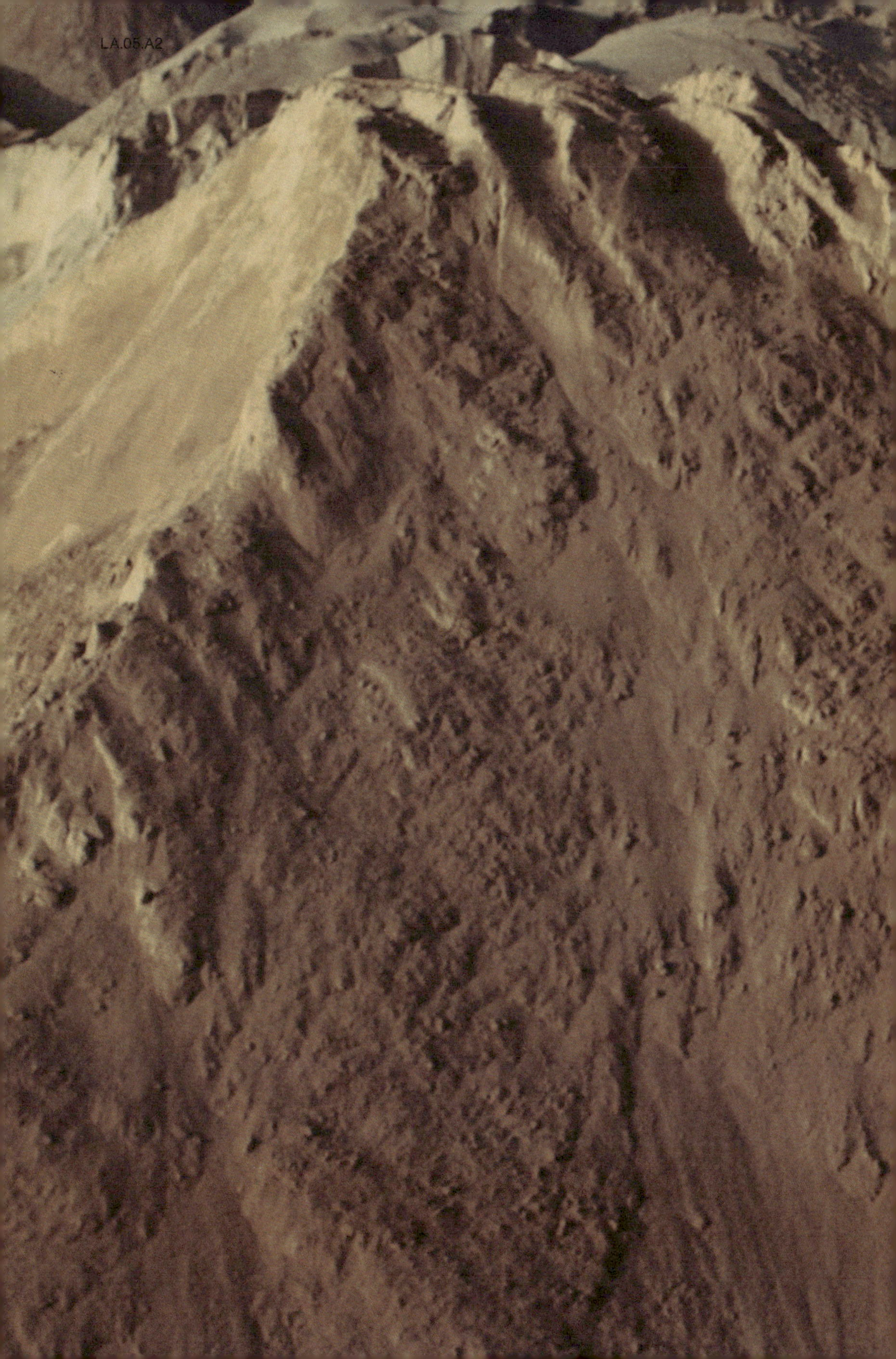
LA.05.A2

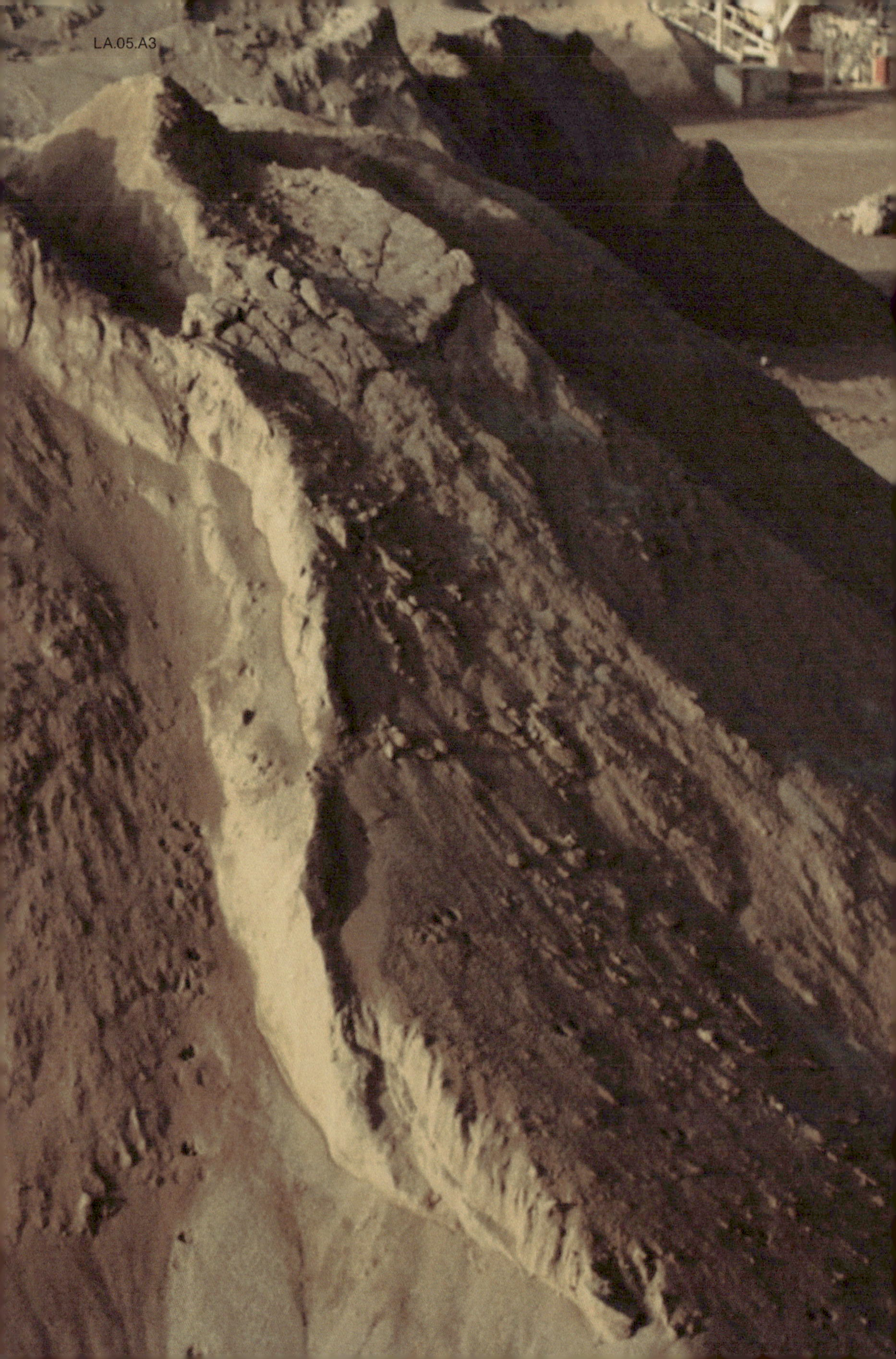
LA.05.A3

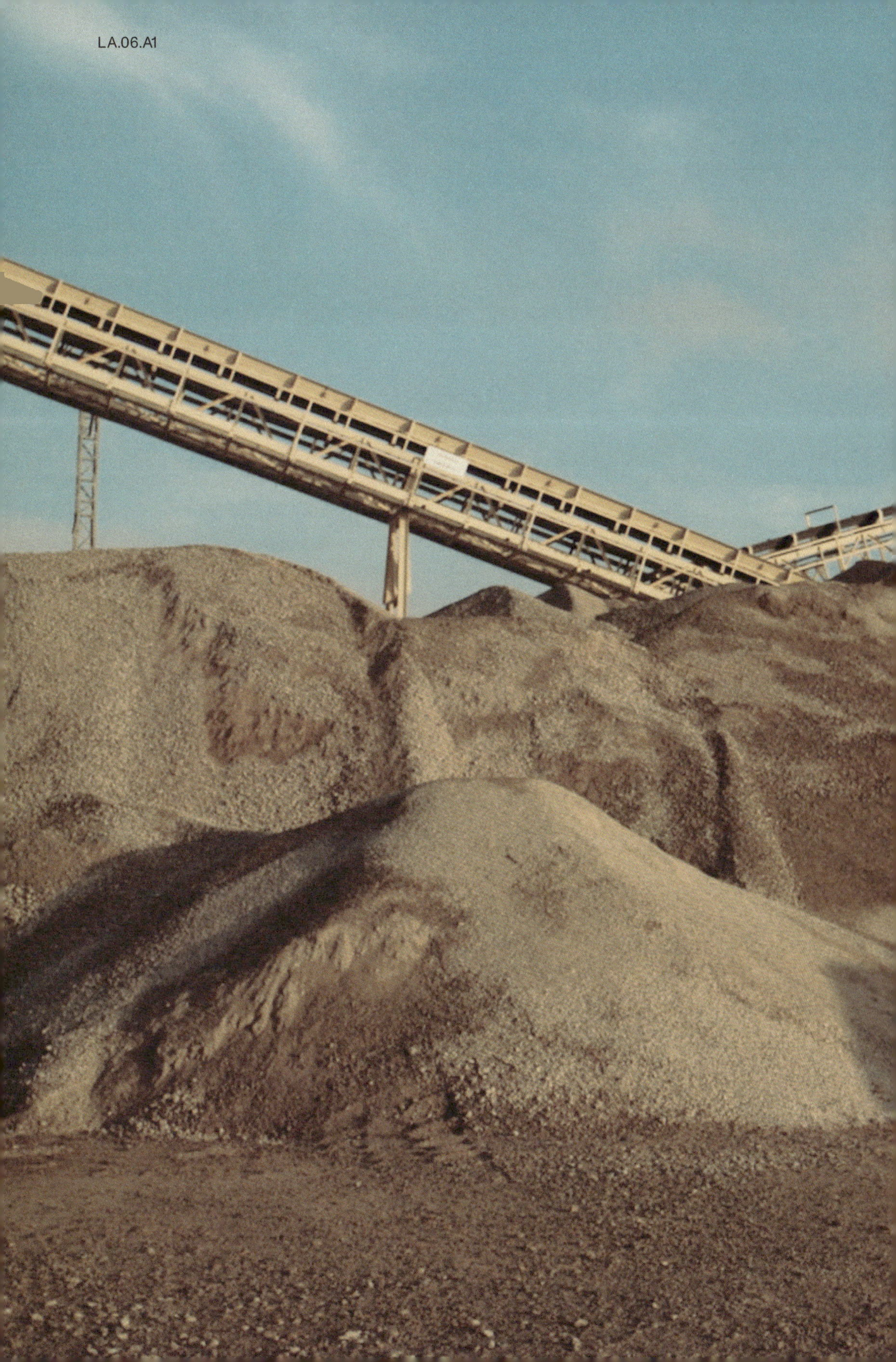
LA.06.A1

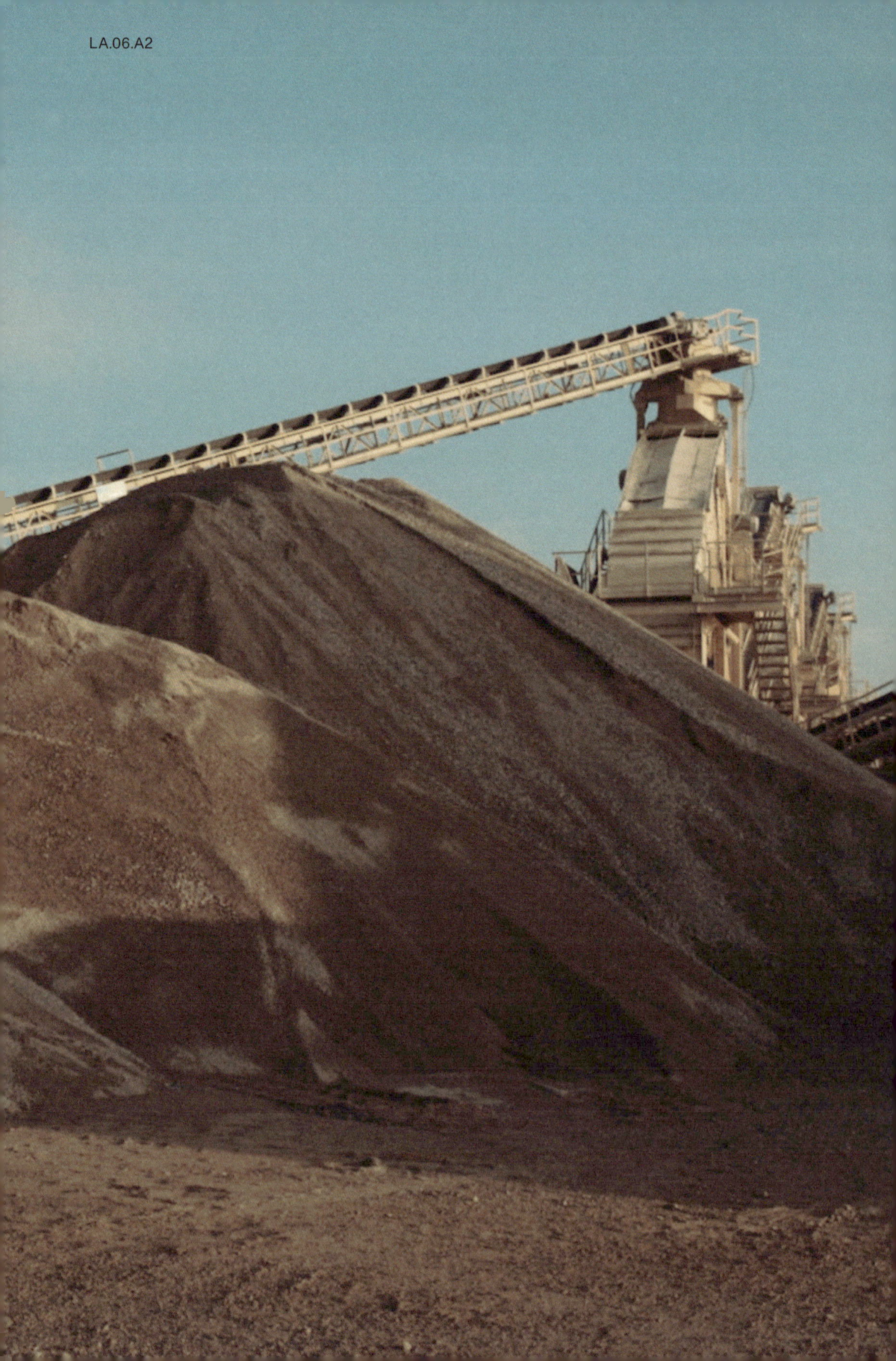
LA.06.A2

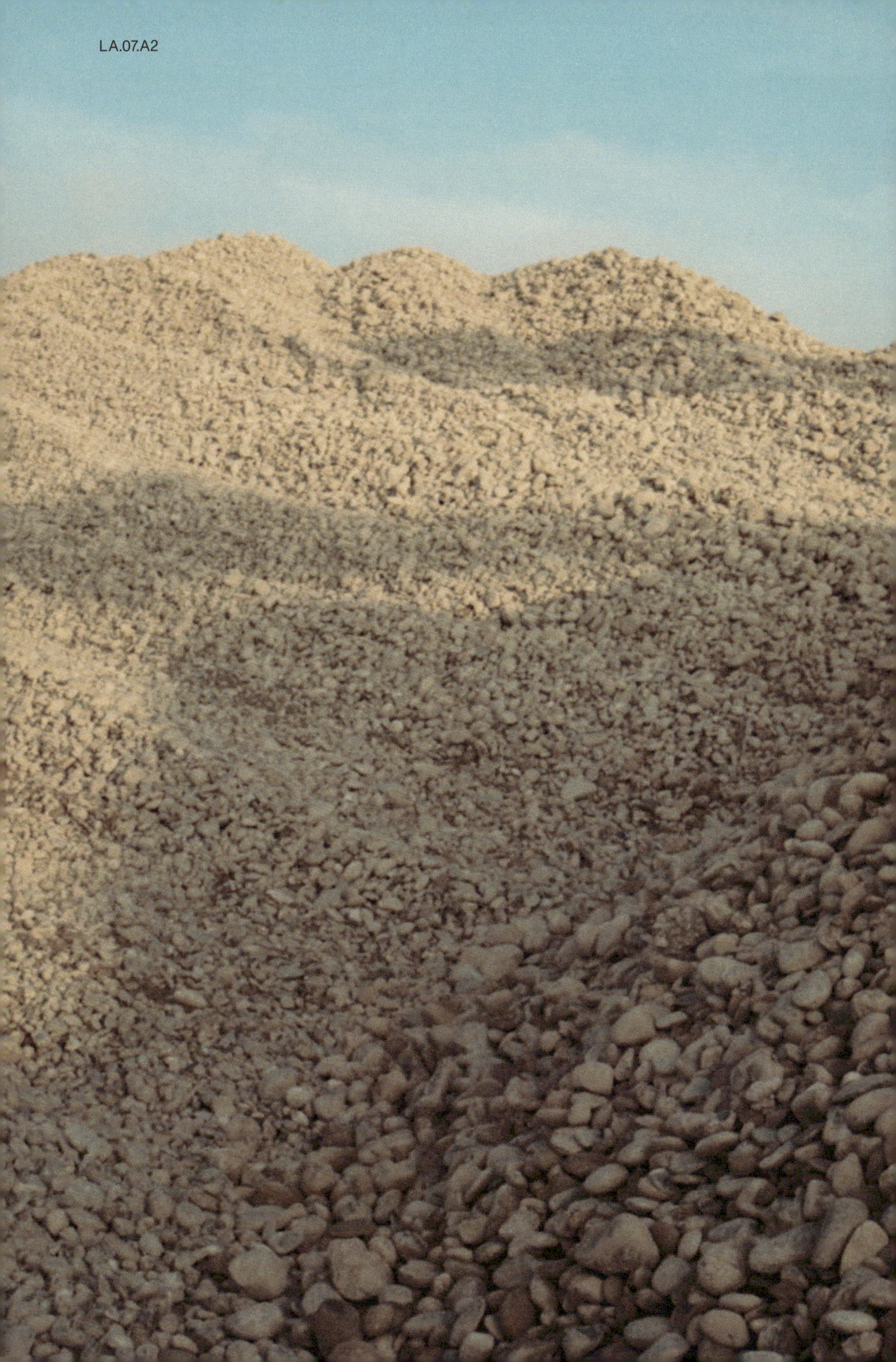

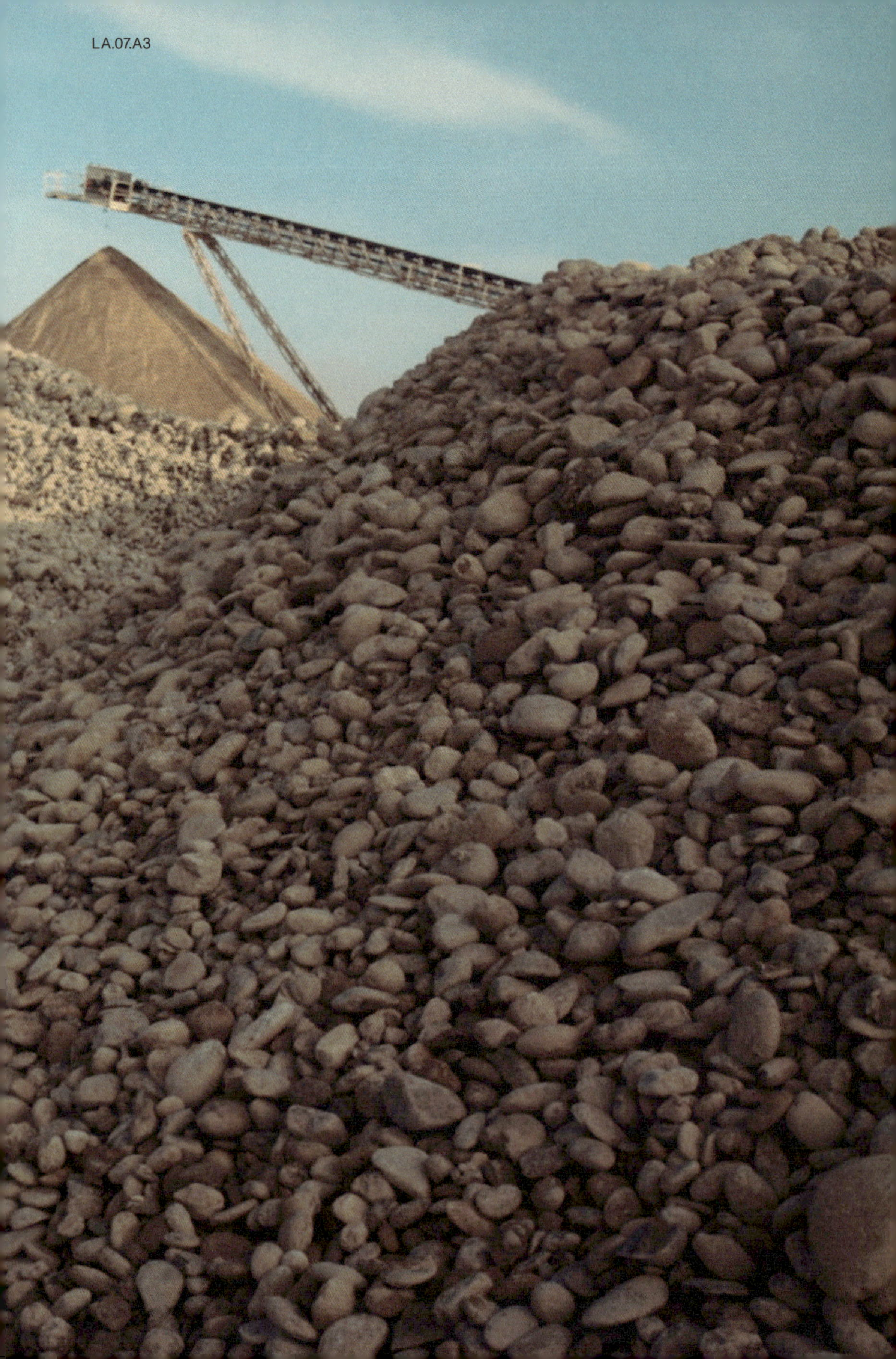
LA.07.A3

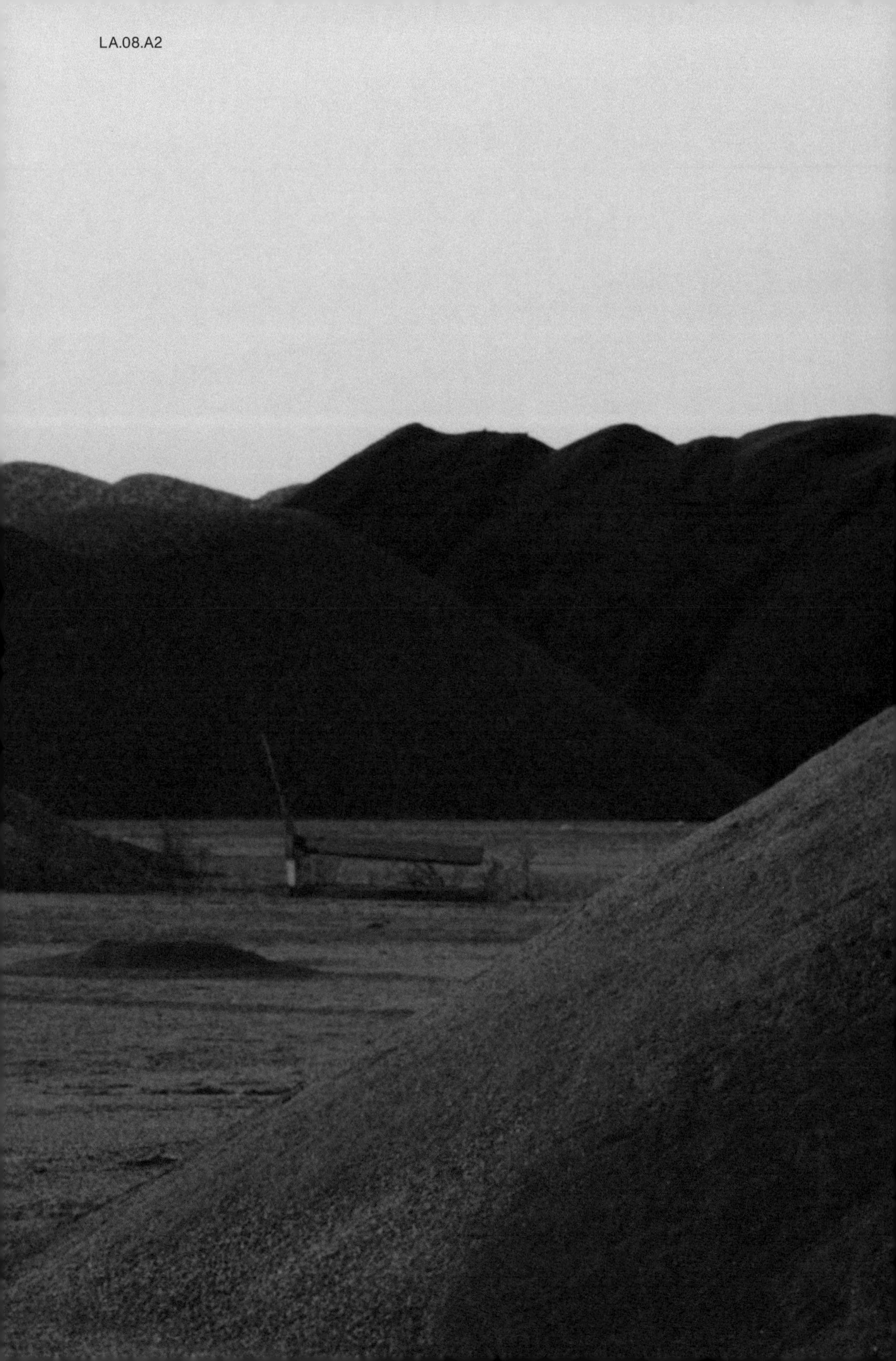
LA.08.A2

LA.08.A3

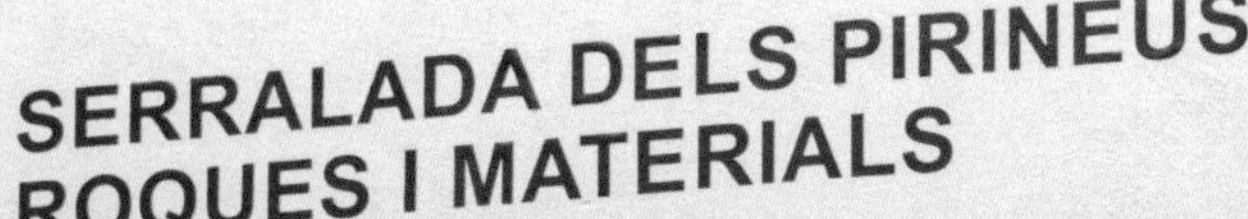

SERRALADA DELS PIRINEUS
ROQUES I MATERIALS

Calcària	213 349 500 036 550 t
Marga	170 362 158 050 000 t
Pissarra	133 112 758 974 000 t
Granit	30 785 079 918 500 t
Gneis	21 128 162 088 000 t
Dolomia	18 075 646 060 050 t
Evaporita	16 217 431 711 800 t
Gres	14 779 869 407 100 t
Flysch	13 018 209 588 000 t
Conglomerat	8 766 169 613 900 t
Gabre	1 073 474 200 310 t
Total	640 668 459 648 210 t

Yana Naidenov

Yana Naidenov

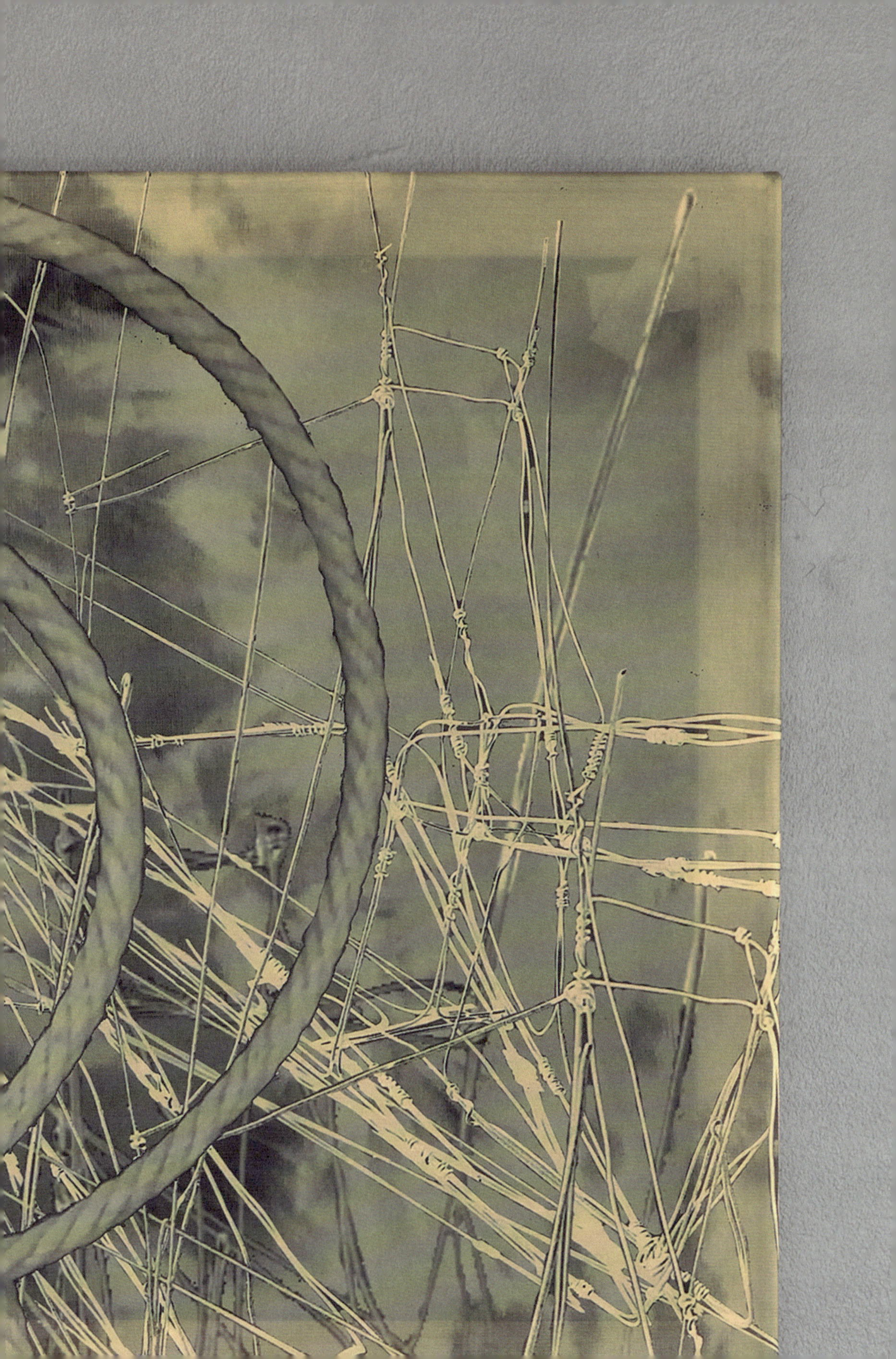

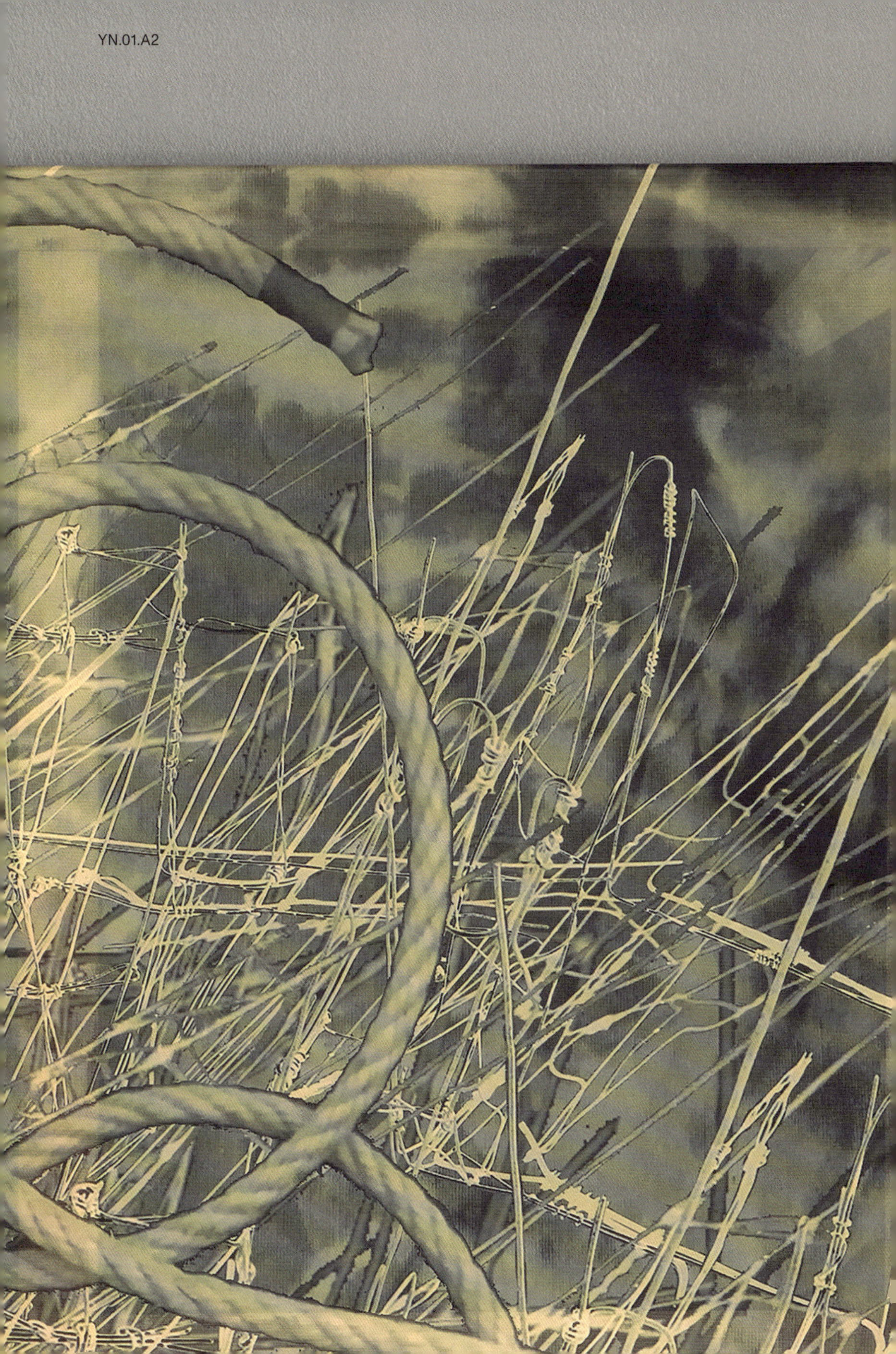

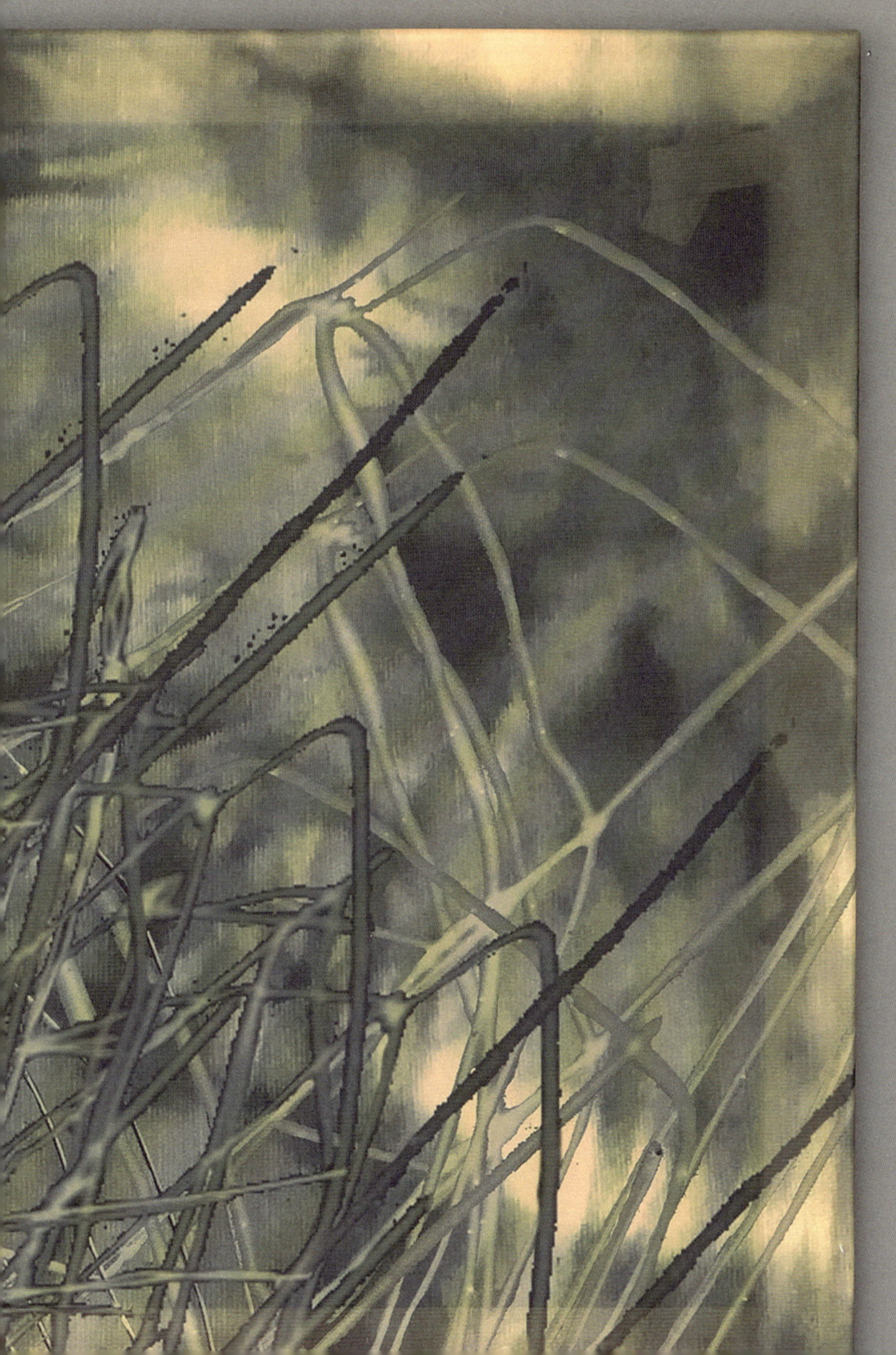

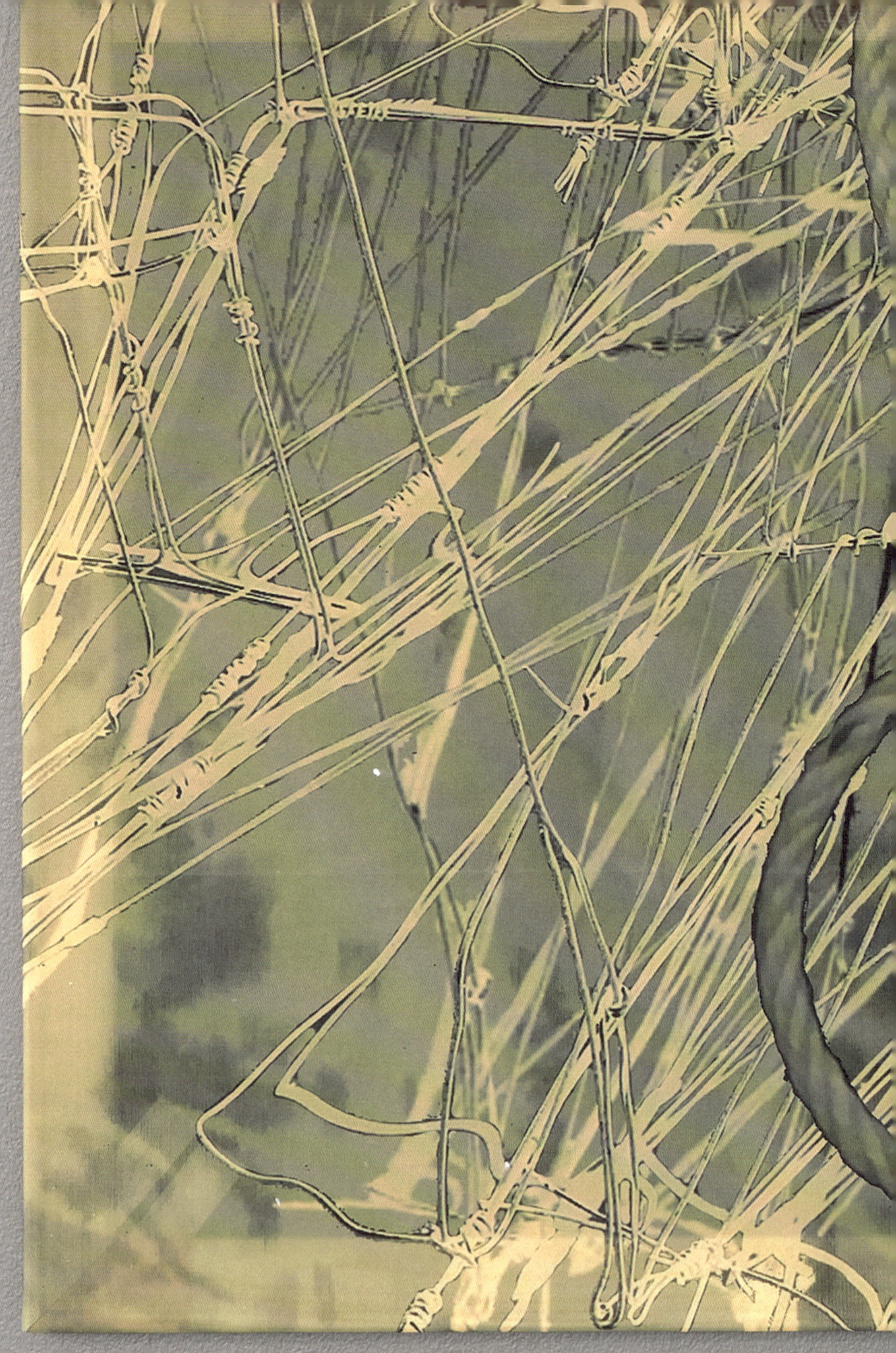

YN.01.B1

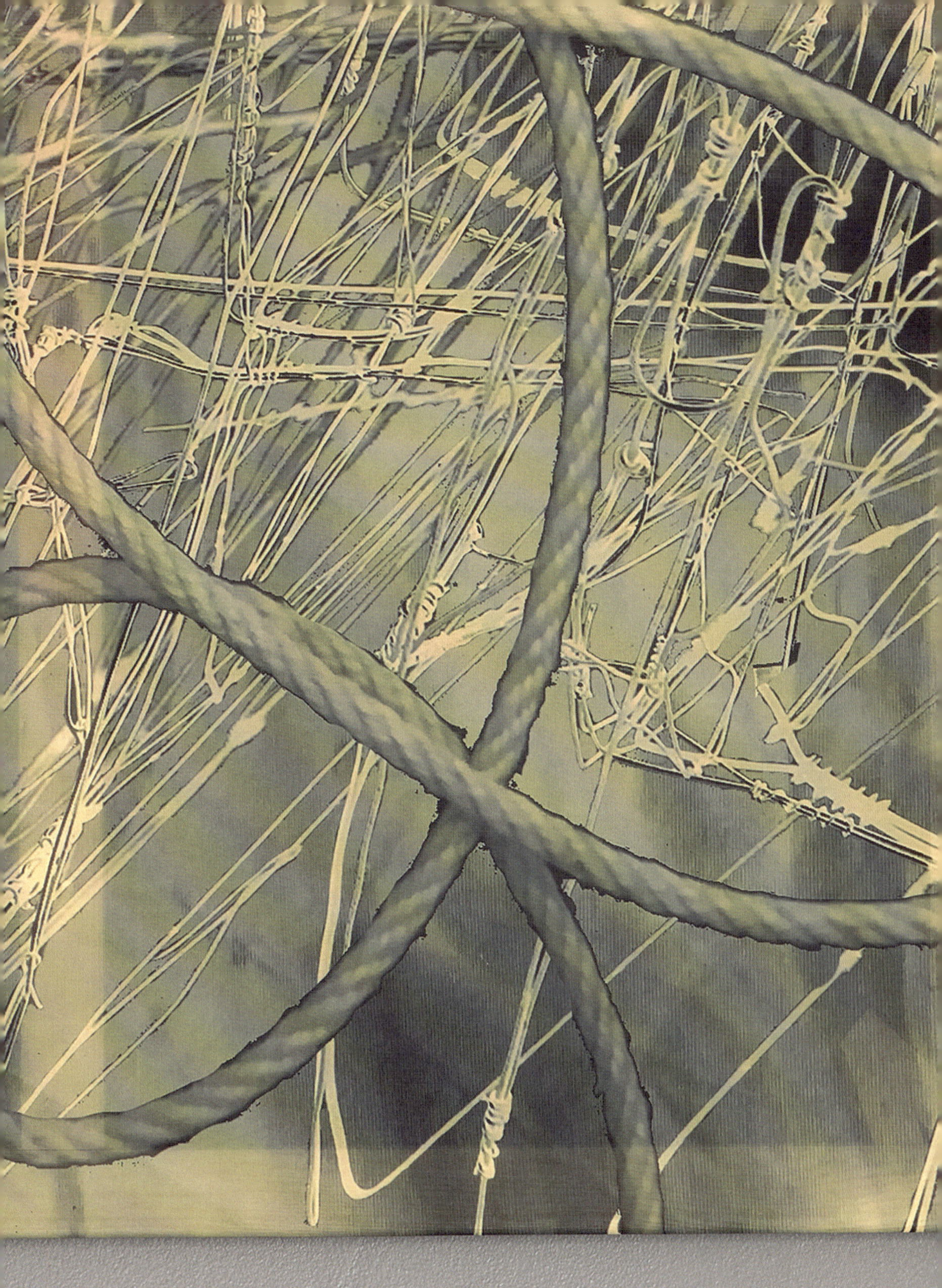

YN.01.B2

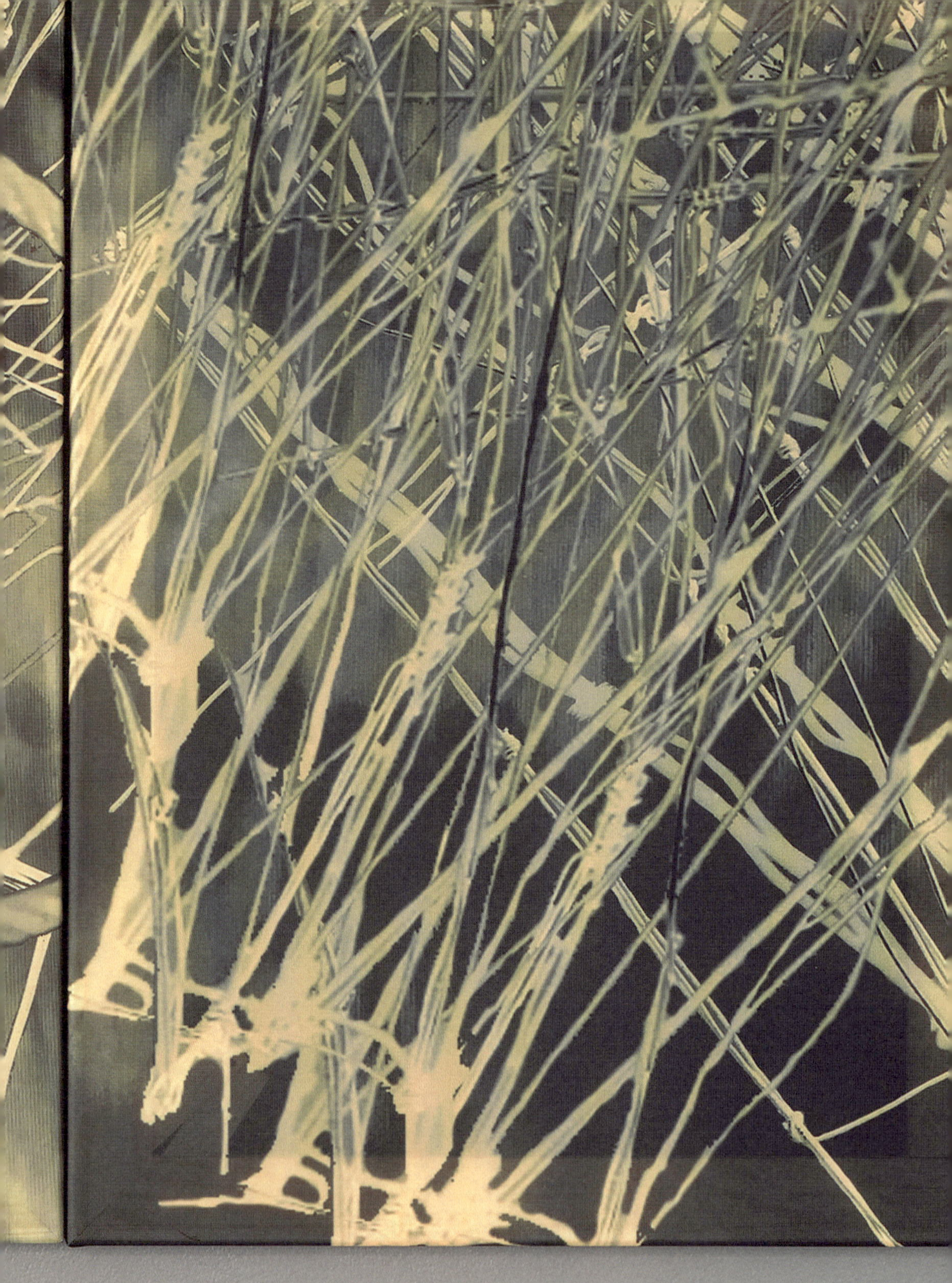

YN.01.B3

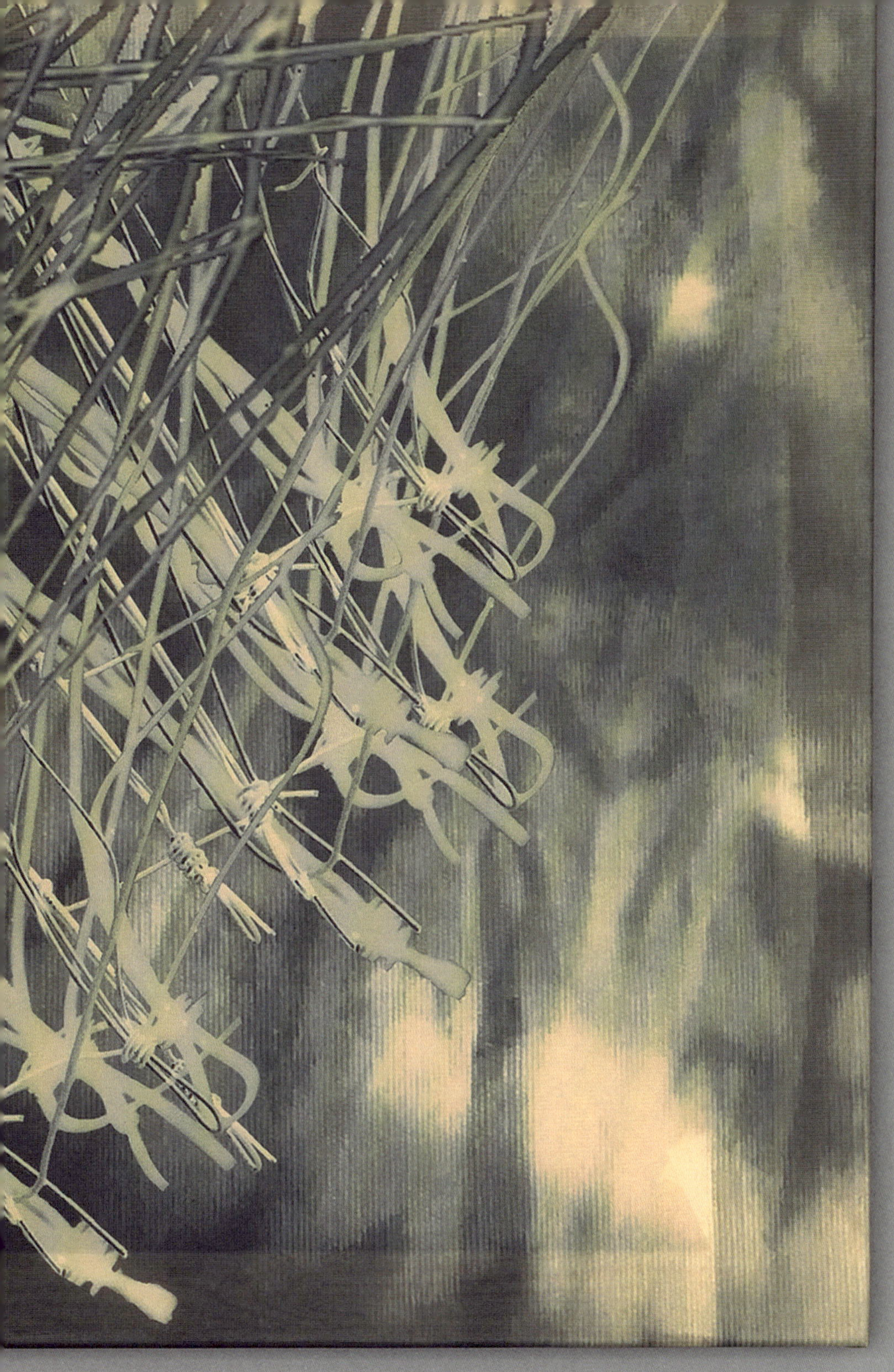

YN.01.B4

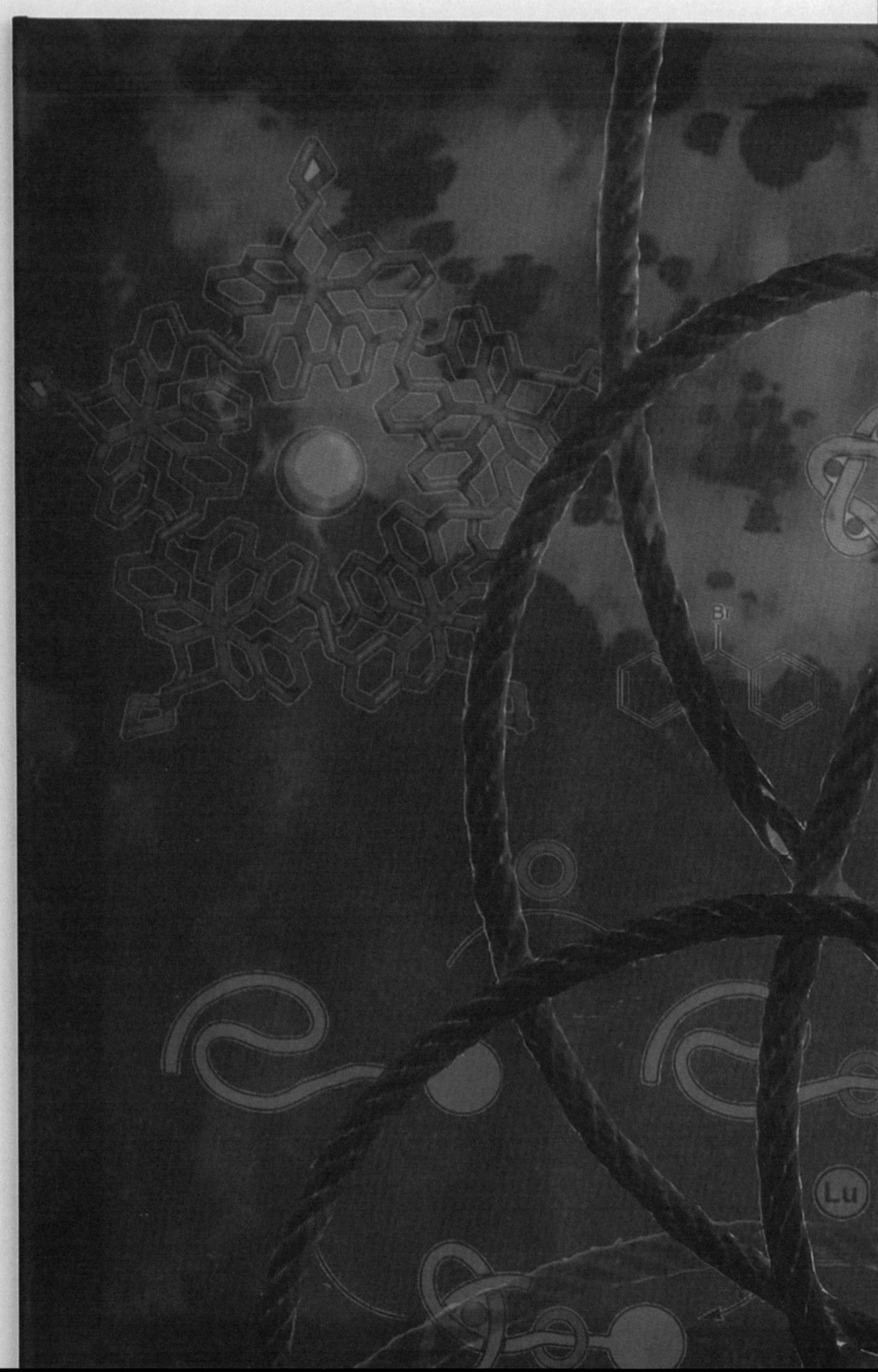

eCN, H₂O
OH
Br
Cu Lu
Cu or Lu

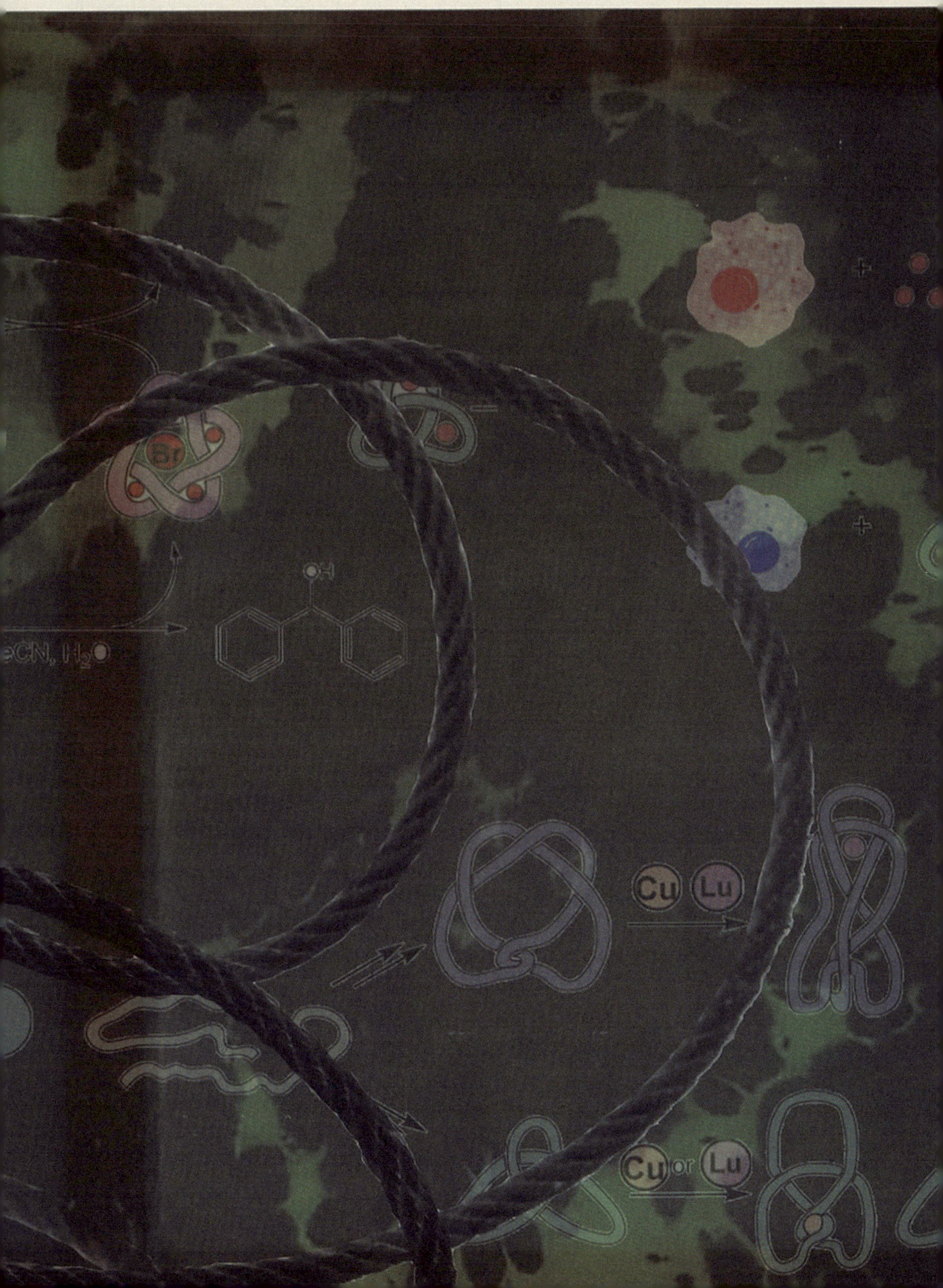

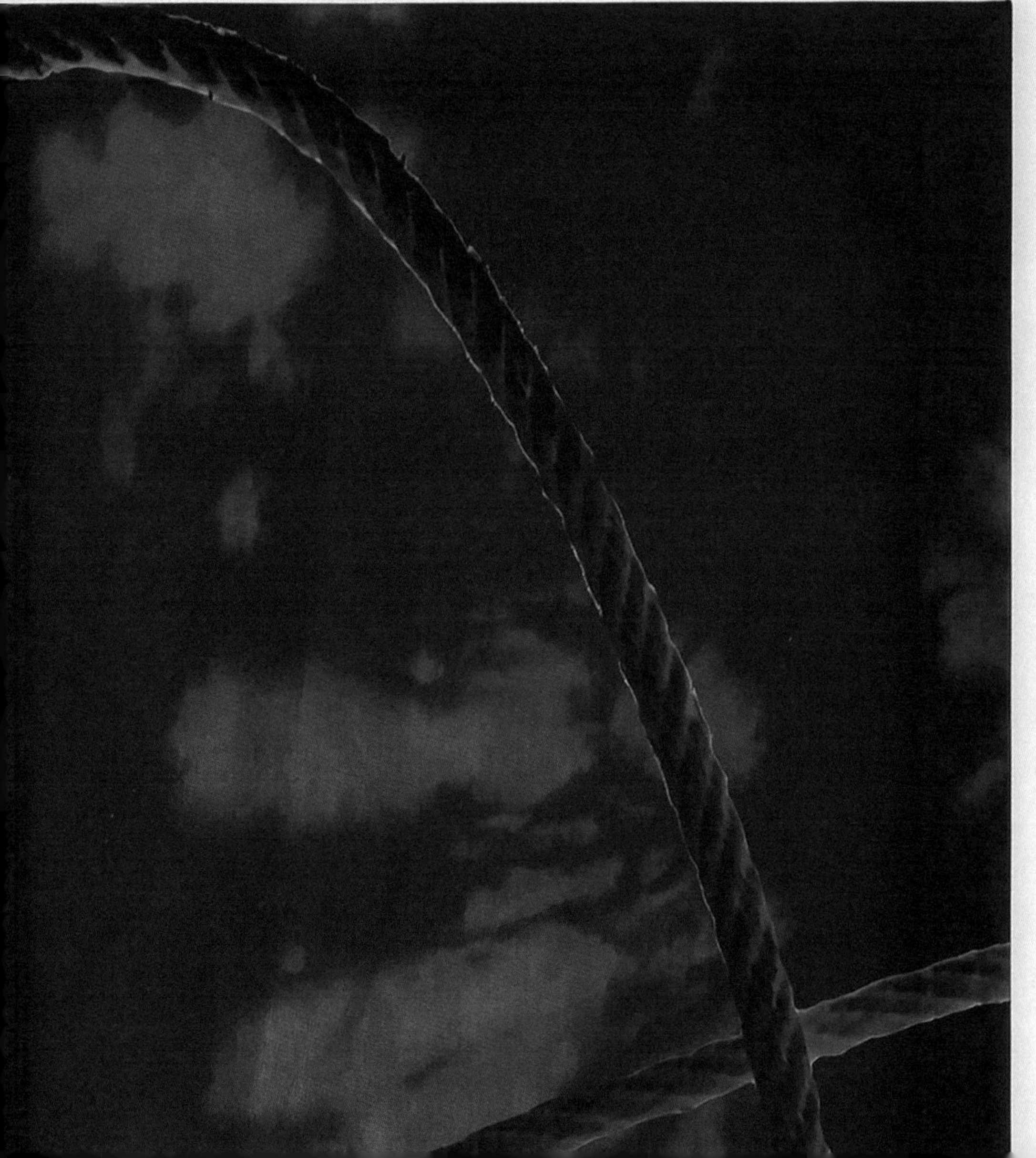

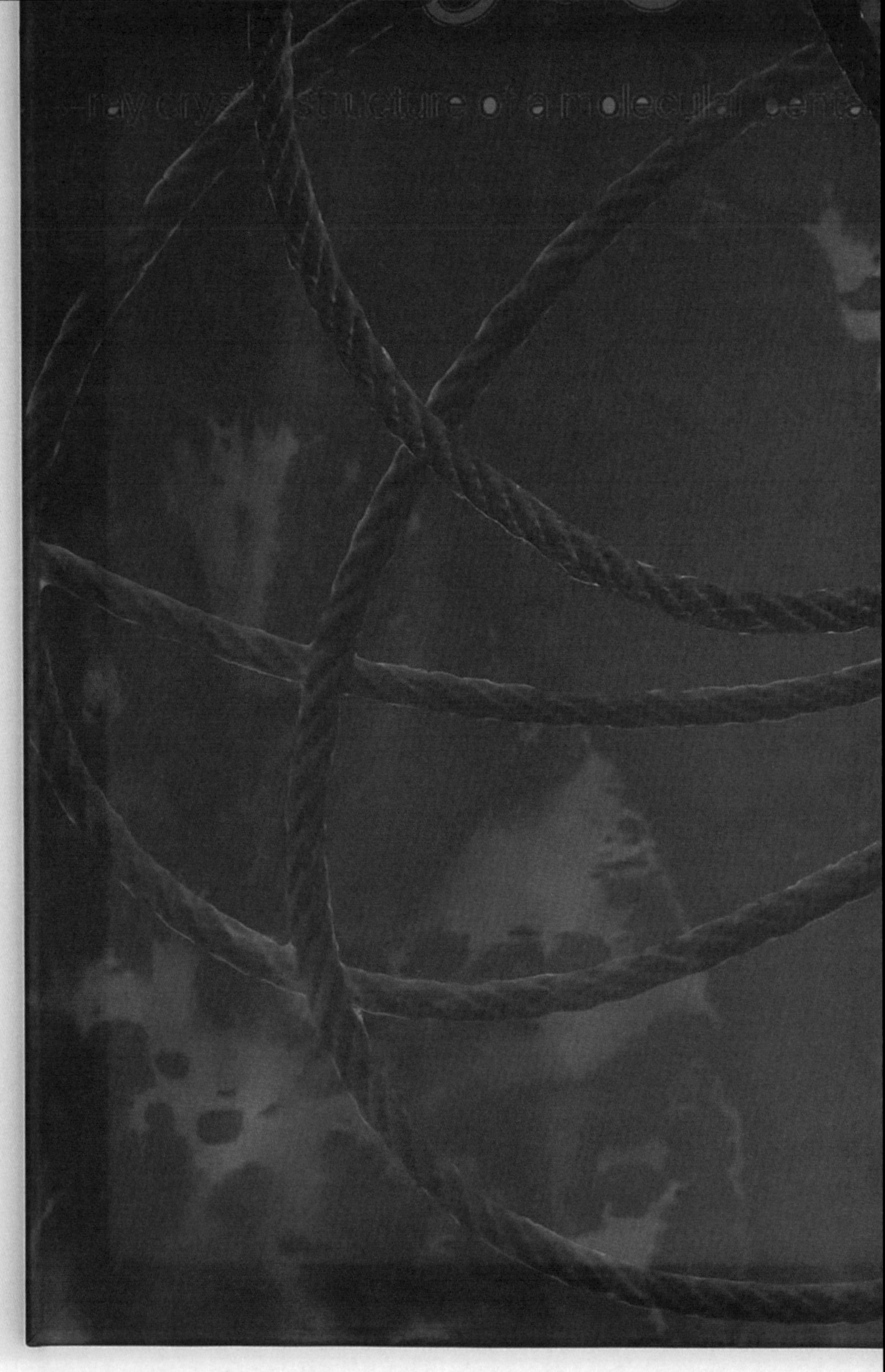

YN.02.B1

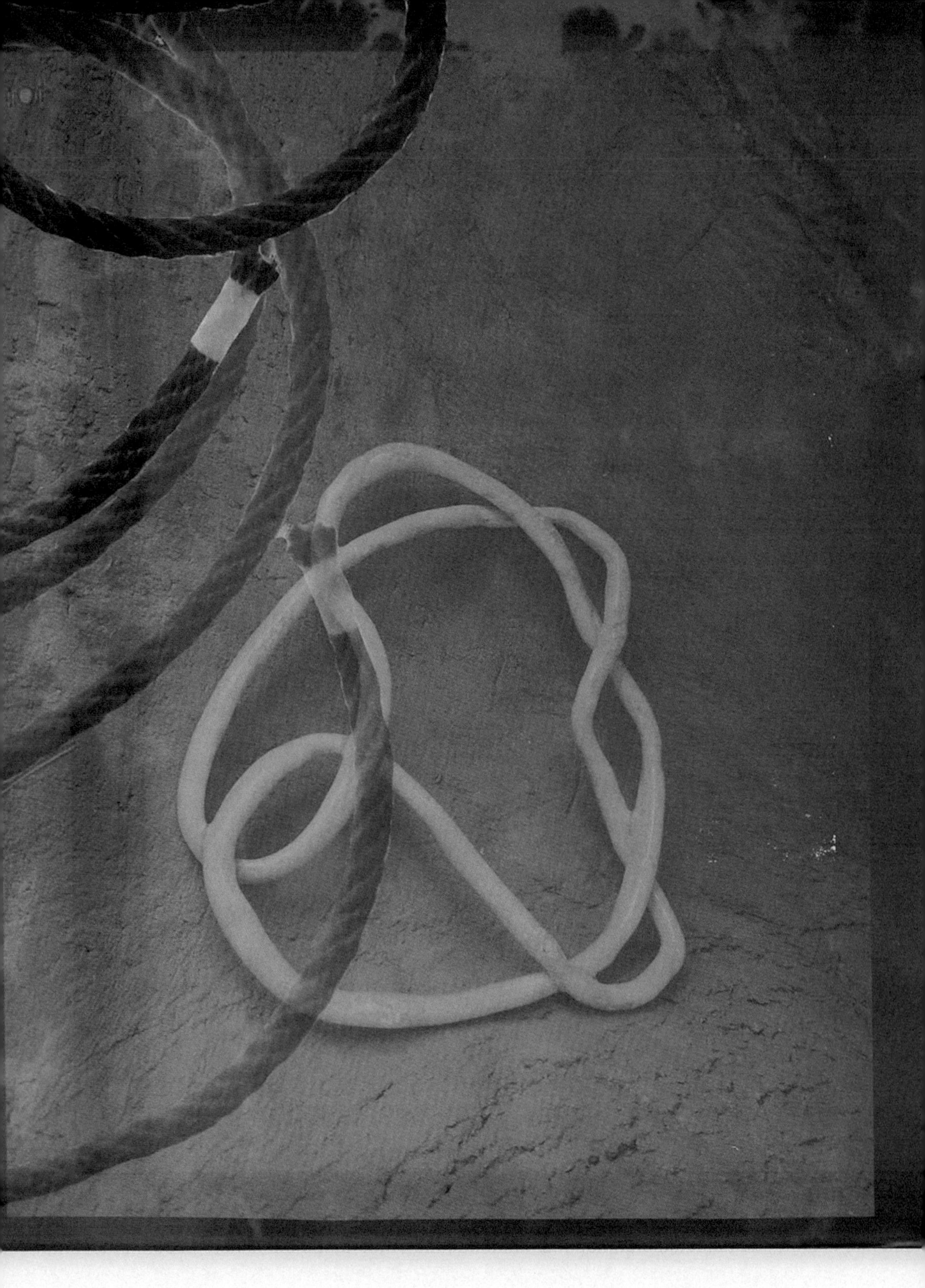

YN.02.B2

YN.02.B3

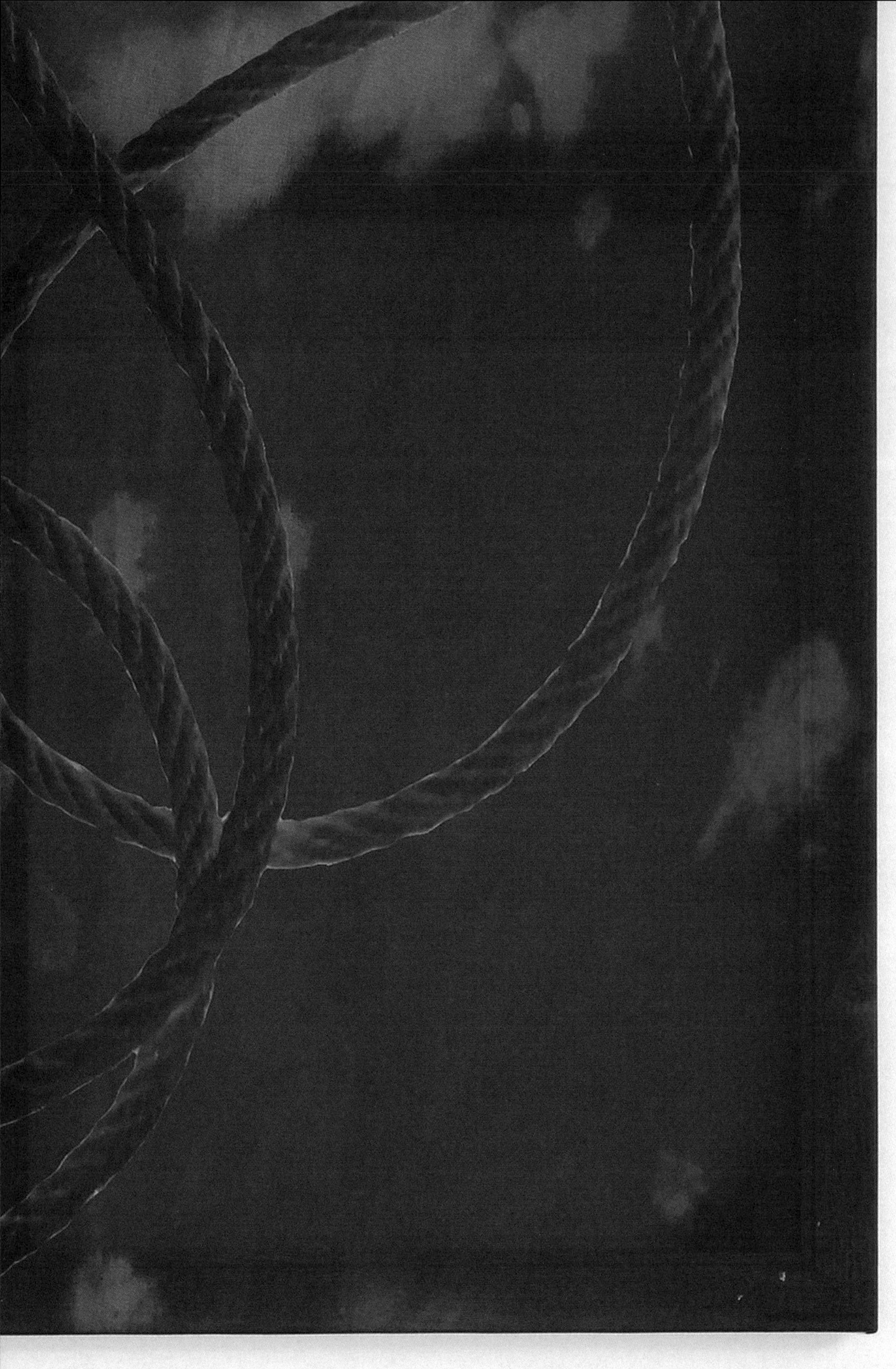

YN.02.B4

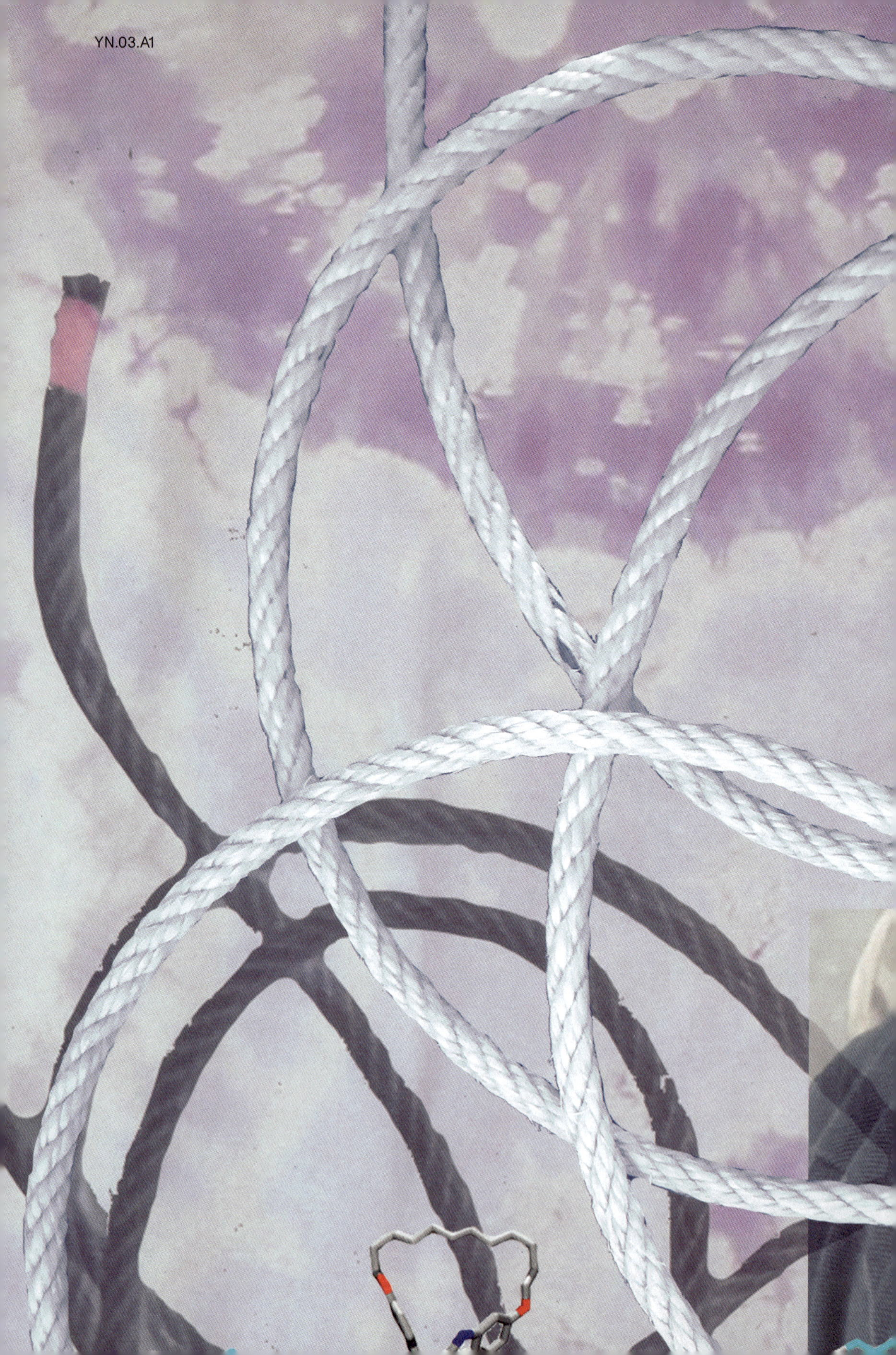

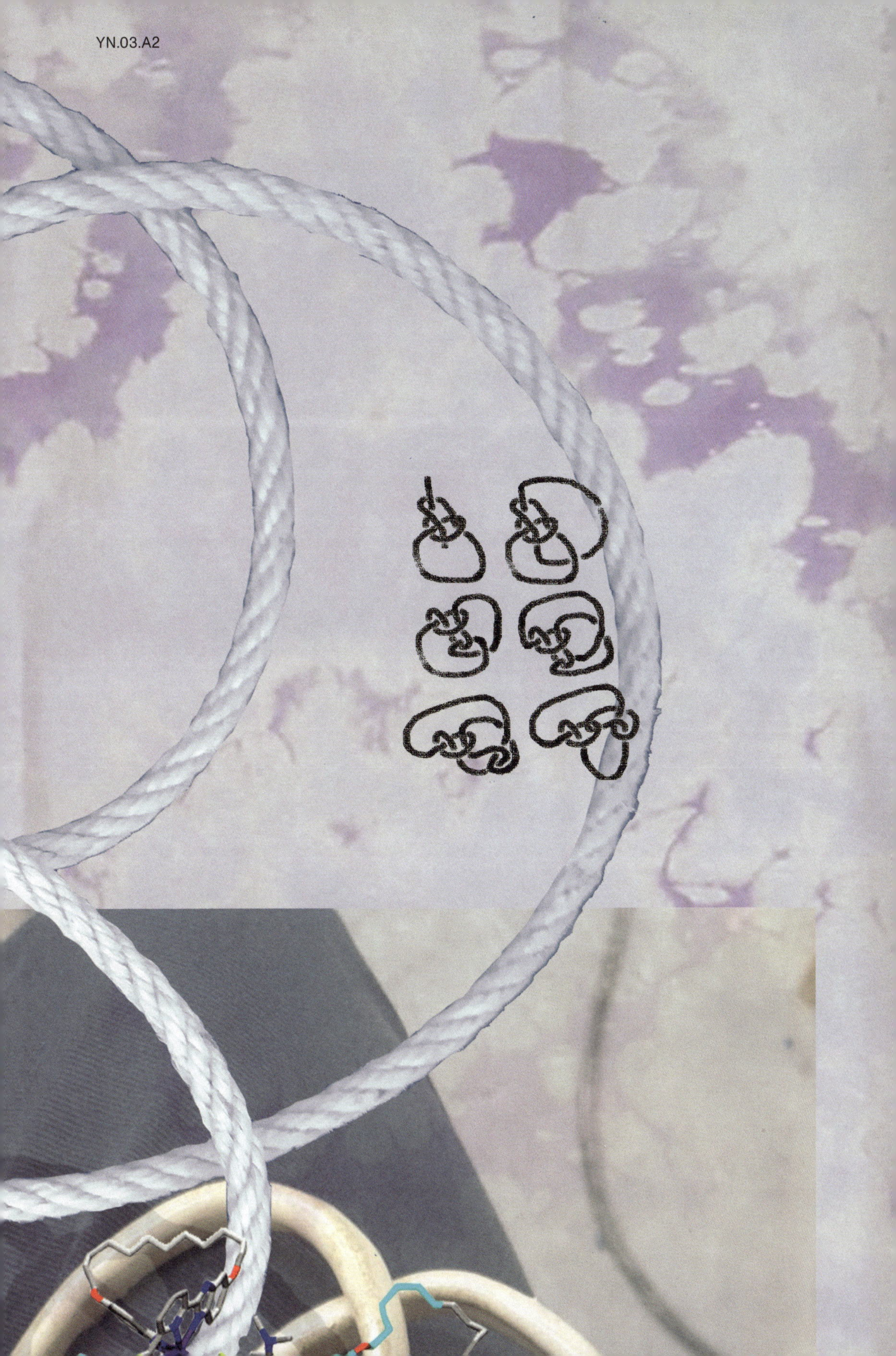

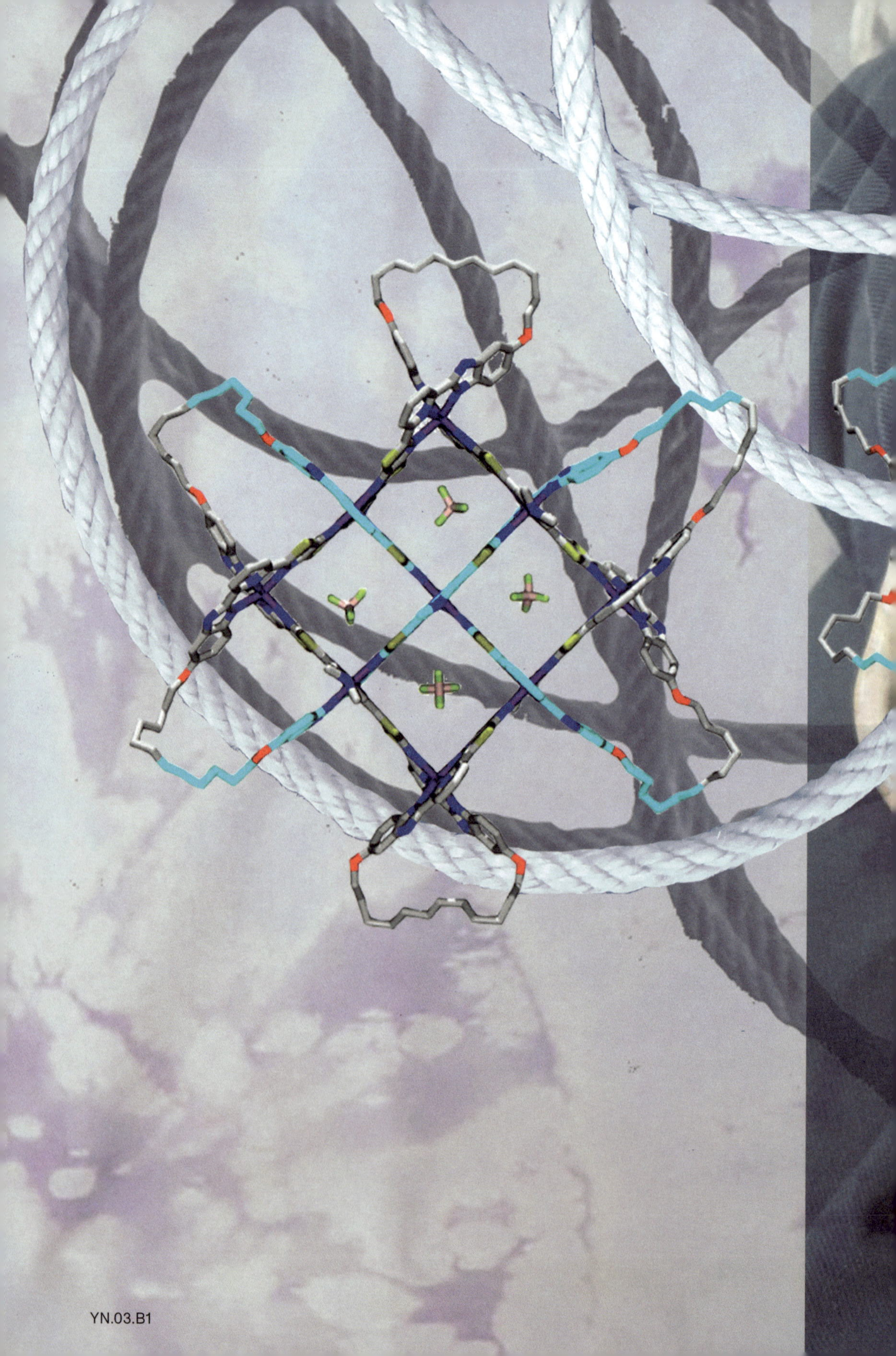

YN.03.B1

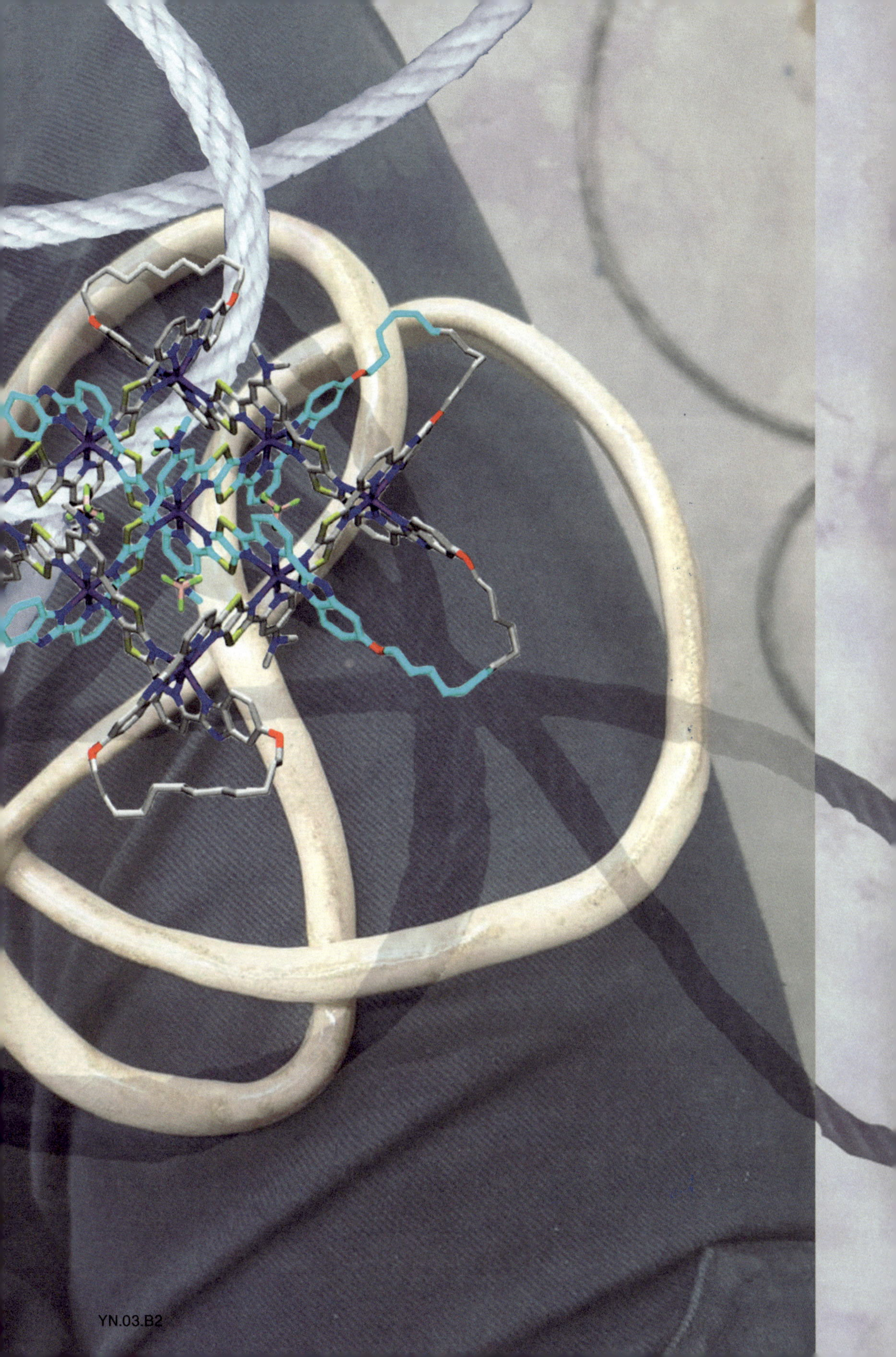

YN.03.B2

SKETCHES
OF TRANSITION

An Atlas on
Growth and Decay

Table of contents

INTRODUCTION

In an age of ecological derangement, major geopolitical shifts and 24/7 neoliberal regimes, the present is a time of complex global transformations. Through their manifold effects, this only becomes manifest and experienceable by the individual on the local level. While the transformations seem to be mainly taking place outside and around us, their effects constantly point at us, questioning our anthropocentric, western and westernized perspectives, until they reveal the role of our human agency—as a species as well as individuals—within them and within our environment at large. Today, we find ourselves in the middle of a transition that does not present itself as a process of overcoming or as the production of the new in avant-garde fashion, but rather as a process demanding that we reinterpret the past and redefine our present (which is characterized by a still incomplete paradigm shift).

Art is an open system that feeds on exchange. Through the work of many contemporary artists, art nowadays becomes the expression of a world that is shared with non-human entities and beings. This offers more intimate perspectives and understandings of our entanglements within the transformations of our uncertain times.

This volume brings together the practices of five different artists in relation to the key concept of transition. Texts, visual documentation and a poem enter into dialogue with each other here, thereby offering the reader a sort of exhibition on the page as an invitation to reflect on our entanglements with external realities.

Gazing through the various apertures of the featured researches, each chapter could be considered a *sketch of transition* in itself, as an annotation on an alternative perspective on the material and visual spheres of our existences. With the same freedom of sketching on a blank paper sheet, the contributions gathered here investigate and probe new modes of production of beauty and wonder.

Maria Barnas

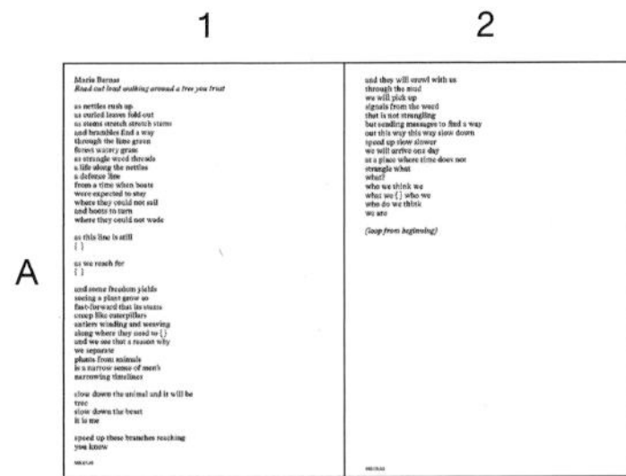

MB.01 *A tree you trust*, 2022, poem

A tree you trust has been first published
on the occasion of the exhibition:
*Enchant embrace them you odd
peninsula – A gathering with love*, for
Kunstfort, which took place between
April 10 and July 10 2022 at Kunstfort
Vijfhuizen in Amsterdam.

Michele Bazzoli

SKETCHES OF TRANSITION

As a visual artist it could turn out to be important to keep an archive, not only as a chronology of your artistic research, but above all because it constitutes a pool of resources from which you can constantly draw inspiration by tracing new paths of meaning, or by interweaving its sources with your current ideas and research findings. This generates input for new work.

In 2019, at the beginning of my master's degree in Visual Arts & Ecology Futures at the St. Joost Master Institute for Visual Cultures, I was diving into my visual archive, which back then was spread across a few notebooks, folders, and hard drives from the previous four years. I went looking for pictures and other visual annotations which could help me to articulate my thoughts and latest research findings in visual form. I focused my research on the intersection of visual arts and the current debate on ecology, and I was seeking to produce a new body of work to give shape to the tensions I saw within it. My theoretical studies were developing around topics such as the Anthropocene (and positions criticizing it), speculative realisms such as new materialism and the philosophical movement of object-oriented ontology (OOO), and in general around human relationships with the nonhuman and the environment, through the work of authors like Bruno Latour, Rosi Braidotti, Donna Haraway, Mark Fisher, Manuel De Landa, and Amitav Gosh. Within this context, my research was driven by the urgency to find a way in which an artwork, with particular regard to sculpture, could offer a more intimate perspective on our entanglement within the transformations that are characterizing our present. How could I do this without having to rely on the specificity of a study case, data analysis or integrated assessment models (IAM)? In other words, I was searching for a way of making art that could abstract from the specificity of localized environments, places, and objects so that it could reflect the more widespread changes of our times and help me understand my own position within these changes.

From that process of scrutinizing my visual archive, two particular images re-emerged. They are snapshots I took with my phone on a sunny afternoon in Zaragoza, around November 2018, when I was strolling with my partner and a friend of hers

at the outskirts of the Spanish city, close to Cuarte de Huerva. A barren and dry area with sparse and low vegetation extends there for kilometers, and given its desert-like appearance her friend sarcastically began referring to this land as La Nada (literally meaning 'the nothingness').

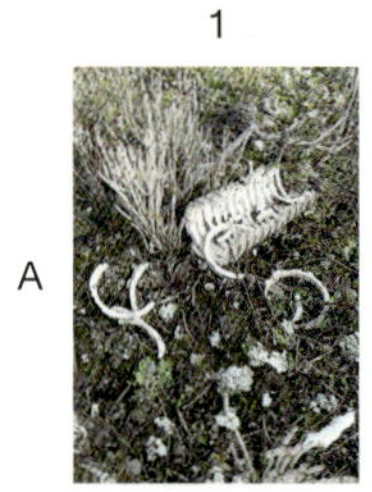

MiB.01   IMG_20181129_105746 (La Nada), Cuarte de Huerva, 2018

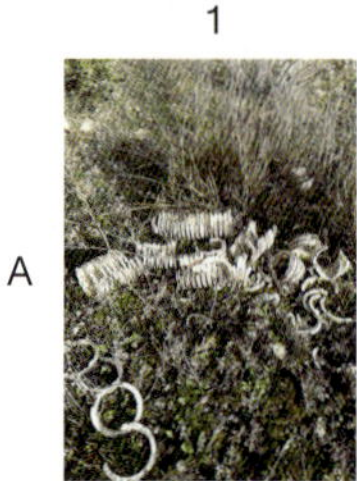

MiB.02   IMG_20181129_105759 (La Nada), Cuarte de Huerva, 2018

The subjects of the photographs are close-up views of the ground in La Nada, depicting the remains of an old broken plastic tube. 'How did it get there,' I wondered when retrieving the pictures two years later. Maybe the tube used to be part of an irrigation system or agricultural machinery. Yet there was almost nothing around us. Although we had not entered that seemingly empty area for more than a few hundred meters, we had to climb a couple of relatively high hills (more like dunes), that kept on multiplying kilometers ahead, to observe the ambiguous nature of this place: there were no crops in sight, nor buildings or fences that demarcated private property; there were no trees, nor plants taller than half a meter; while at that moment nobody else was there. For some reason, however, it did not seem to be a completely unaltered natural place. On the ground one could distinguish numerous varieties of shrubs, minerals, different shades of lichens, animal traces and, scattered here and there, debris of various, mostly industrial objects. Walking on the slope of one of those arid dunes, several things creaked under the weight of our steps: branches and twigs, soft dry clods of dirt, white grainy stones of various shapes, and some plastic pieces such as those from the photographs. Exposed to the sun and dry winds that often blow in that region, the plastic had lost its elasticity, was drying up, and becoming as fragile as the bones of a decomposed animal carcass. As if we found ourselves adrift in an immense reservoir, it seemed as if these plastic pipes had appeared on the soil of that semi-deserted area as a result of long-term natural changes, such as the retreat of a great ancient

                    Michele Bazzoli

tide. Given its ambiguous nature, La Nada seemed to mark a space at the intersection between the city and more natural areas, a transitional place that tacitly kept a record of the entanglement of our human activities and the processes of the earth.

It was clear how, unlike what happens in the physical structures of our human-made environments, in this kind of wilderness materials do not serve any symbolic, social or political function, as it fully embodies the ecosystems in which it participates, while flowing through innumerous and unique aggregations. I found it fascinating how 'out there' matter aggregates and disintegrates all the time, its shapes continuously changing without any intentional hierarchies. Without knowledge of any physical boundaries between each other, these material transformations are governed by natural and chemical processes that, together with the elements, define its continuous becoming. Existence permeates things in different states and degrees of intensity. Depending on our relationship with them, we often recognize what is more important, which things contain more 'being' or meaning than what we care for less. In *The Labyrinth* the French philosopher, writer and anthropologist Georges Bataille pays particular attention to how "not only do [material] states have a variable intensity, but different beings 'are' unequally. A dog that runs and barks seems 'to be' more than a mute and clinging sponge, the sponge more than the water in which it lives, an influential man more than a vacant passerby."[1]

While our anthropocentric perspectives don't seem to find a concrete hold on reality, our activities cannot but alter the natural processes that govern it, creating repercussions for long timespans. The fragmented and scattered plastic debris in La Nada, a place almost completely devoid of anthropization, seemed to record how far such repercussions can propagate into the material reality, suggesting how one could hypothetically reread the latter entirely starting from the intensity levels of these repercussions. In fact, despite the immeasurable ontological distance between a discarded plastic tube and that barren area, they are much more interconnected than it seems. In particular, I had to think about how the material of that scattered object was going through yet another transition, both its physical state and shape: from a portion of organic substance that became petroleum resulting from millions of years of sedimentation processes, to then

be shaped by humans into polymeric material (probably PVC),
and then to become an object for common use. Finally, and not
without a veil of irony, it came to resemble the bones of some
strange animal species and is destined to dissolve during a process
of biodegradation (lasting at least 450 years) and perhaps to
be incorporated into living organisms once again. These elements
seemed to have been teleported here from another dimension,
and at the same time they paradoxically seem to belong to this
place as an endemic species. La Nada seems to attest to the already
evident effects of our pervasive dance with Gaia.

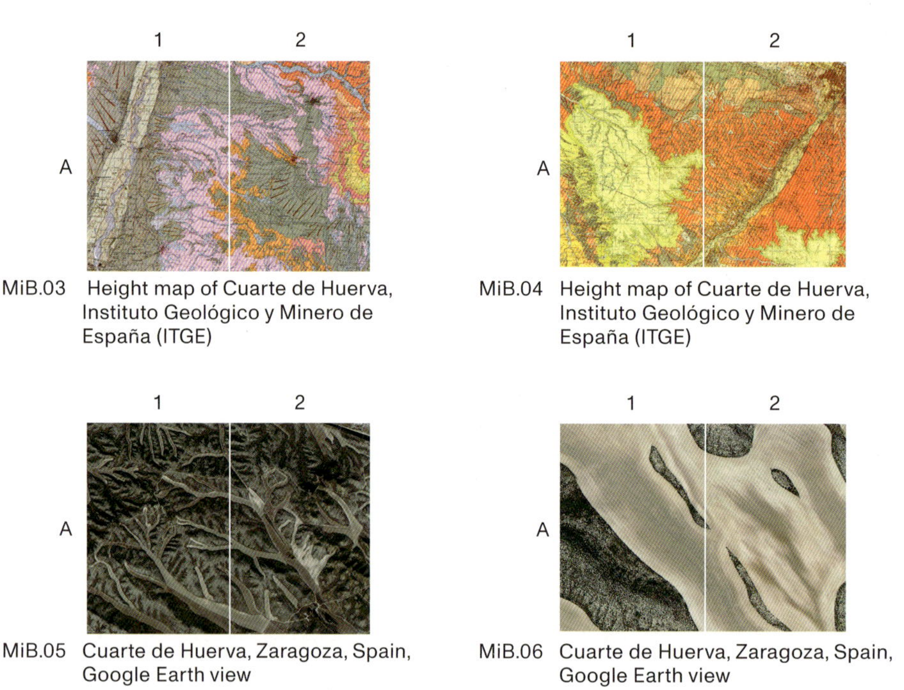

MiB.03   Height map of Cuarte de Huerva,
Instituto Geológico y Minero de
España (ITGE)

MiB.04   Height map of Cuarte de Huerva,
Instituto Geológico y Minero de
España (ITGE)

MiB.05   Cuarte de Huerva, Zaragoza, Spain,
Google Earth view

MiB.06   Cuarte de Huerva, Zaragoza, Spain,
Google Earth view

Leaving Zaragoza by plane we saw something that can only be
observed by zooming out from the ground level: from the air
La Nada revealed an interesting constellation. Around the dunes
we had traversed, there appeared a dense and intricate succes-
sion of wide sinuous shapes, similar to hermatypic corals or
nerve endings. Due to the scalelessness that places often assume
when seen from above, these shapes even resembled silhouettes
of strange unicellular organic beings. They extended as far as
the eye could see and were bound only by small towns and a few
roads connecting them, sometimes following and sometimes
abruptly interrupting their tortuous course. What is the cause
of this unusual constellation? What relationship did it have with
the towns and cities within it, if any? After having done some

        Michele Bazzoli

research on the area south of the capital of Aragon and thanks
to the expertise of the University of Zaragoza and the Escuela
Superior de Diseño de Aragón, I learned it is a typical constellation of the region, whose origins date back to ancient processes of
land transformation. Milions of years ago Aragon was a shallow
sea isolated from the Mediterranean: the Ebro Basin, the bottom
of which was about 800 meters above sea level, much higher than
the current topography. Its endorheic regime favored evapora-
tion, which over time generated gypsum rocks such as alabaster,
a unique type of stone that today is exported all over the world—
the same kind of stone many fragments of which we noticed
while walking there. By the end of the Miocene, erosion and
river incision reconnected the basin to the Mediterranean Sea.
As a result of this process the valleys that today characterize the
area with their articulated reliefs began to form. The Ebro Basin
gradually transformed into the homonymous river that crosses
the city of Zaragoza today. The fluvial incision producing these
flat-bottomed valleys, locally known as 'vales', filled them with
fertile sedimentary deposit, so these valleys were perfect for agricultural purposes. Thus, the giant drawing-like areas correspond
to the plantable areas, which are used nowadays for cultivating
cereal plants.

I was lucky that I retrieved these two photographs, so rich in
information and yet so abstract: two snapshots of vivid memo-
ries that portray these scattered fragments of carcass-like objects,
in slow and continuous decay until they find a new life in future
aggregates of matter. These images became an important reference for the process that led me to create the sculptural installation *Sketches of Transition*. In early 2020 I began developing
a new body of work starting from the two photographs of La
Nada, inspired by how the plastic tube resembled animal remains.
Reflecting on the reason why two years earlier I had instinctively
photographed the plastic debris, I found that the resemblance
concealed a deeper meaning than mere visual similarity. More
than similitude it seemed to suggest metaphor: a decaying plastic
tube is like the ribbed cage of a dead animal's endoskeleton. This
clearly human-made object resembled the remains of a non-human
being. As if its state of ruination signaled the apex of the transition that every human-made object goes through during decay,
gradually losing its form and returning to the humus that makes
up the substrate of our material reality. Thinking through the

                    SKETCHES OF TRANSITION

materiality of the debris allowed me to distance myself from its external appearance and to focus on the evocative power of corporeal reminiscences, which in my eyes evoked oddly poetic evidence of our physical entanglement within the natural environment. Back then I was reading philosopher Graham Harman's *Object-Oriented Ontology*, which proposes a particular form of realism and a non-anthropocentric perspective, rejecting the privileging of human existence over the existence of non-human objects. I especially dwelt on what he wrote about metaphor. In a short but relevant passage, Harman explains how he considers this figure of speech as the clearest example of a non-linear form of cognition.

Taking into consideration an essay on metaphor by the Spanish philosopher José Ortega y Gasset, he analyzes how the latter considers the metaphor as an object that, like a work of art, "affords the peculiar pleasure we call esthetic by making it *seem* that the inwardness of things, their executant reality – that is the Kantian noumena – is opened to us." Gasset takes the following metaphor as an example: 'the cypress is like the ghost of a dead flame'. And while the first thing that comes to mind is similarity in shape, just like the plastic tubes and the animal ribbed cage, he argues how a metaphor satisfies because it allows us to grasp an essence that is more profound and significant than mere resemblance may suggest. Any external similarity between objects or phenomena in a metaphor is indeed generally so unsubstantial that it just suffices as pretext. Reflecting on this, Harman writes that "on the basis of their inessential identity, we assert an absolute identity. Yet this is absurd, impossible. The two objects initially repel one another. As a result, we have the annihilation of what [cypress and flame] are as practical images. When they collide with one another they crack their hard carapaces and the internal matter, in a molten state, acquires the softness of plasm, ready to receive a new form and struc-ture."[2] What Harman means is that a succesful metaphor enables us to experience a new entity that somehow combines both sides of the comparison.

Fascinated by my reading about the evocative power of a 'simple' figure of speech like the metaphor, and by the expressiveness of the images of that fragmented object in La Nada, I began to ponder about the use of metaphors in artistic creation. In particular, I began to imagine the possibility of combining several visual

                    Michele Bazzoli

metaphors at once, so that a work could 'break the hard carapaces' of different objects and dimensions and melt their internal matter together. Fusing and recasting its form simultaneously into a multiplicity of shapes, the artwork would embody an image in which the objects of different metaphors are intertwined together, dialoguing and annihilating each other at the same time. Growth and decay, bones and flesh, body and environment, object and architecture, natural and artificial elements, the human and non-human. Researching ways to visualize my own entanglement within the transformations of our present I focused on my relation with all these dimensions, by layering shapes and materials that could represent them metaphorically, in a process that in reality was also composed of subtraction.

What resulted was mostly an abstract image, which would refer to multiple imageries and objects by means of visual metaphors and similarities, and avoid them at the same time. In this chain of references the artwork seems to be temporarily decentralized, on a visual level, by expanding its essence through all the images its metaphors evoke, to then recompose itself in the finitude of the materials it is made of.

Today it is becoming more and more evident how everything on Earth is interconnected, on material as well as immaterial levels, and how nothing can exist without at the same time contaminating and being contaminated by other things and beings. The body does not exist independently of the spaces it inhabits and the objects it interacts with, just as the latter do not exist without the production systems that generate them nor do such systems exist outside historical, economical and political contexts. Everything also has its environmental impact, the effects of which are translated on the body, which cannot exist independently of any 'external environment'. All the elements always exist in relation to permanent technological and scientific developments, global warming, or the current geological era, the so-called Anthropocene.

How to perceive these interconnections? How to visualize our entanglement within these phenomena, which are so much larger than ourselves? According to philosopher Timothy Morton, larger-than-life phenomena are 'hyperobjects': entities too large and extended in time and space to be observed in their entirety, but with which we are constantly interacting. Morton, following

the OOO philosophical movement, defines the hyperobject by attributing to it a series of specific ontological characteristics: in addition to being a *non-local* entity, the hyperobjects is *viscous*, such as global warming, which "never stops sticking to you, no matter where you move on Earth. [...] Global warming is not a function of our measuring devices. Yet because it's distributed across the biosphere and beyond, it's very hard to see as a unique entity. And yet, there it is, raining on us, burning down on us, quaking the Earth, spawning gigantic hurricanes."[3]

Our existence cannot be defined outside of our societies, the material reality that surrounds us, and the hyperobjects with which we share time and space. To me, it is precisely this evident and total co-existence and co-presence, paradoxical some times, of everyone and everything that defines contemporaneity as such: being contemporary is not only a synonym for existing in the present time, or after (post-)modernity, nor does it denote a particular type of relationship with one's own time. First and foremost, being contemporary defines what happens when humans become aware of their mutual co-existence in time and space, and of their co-presence and interdependence with all that is non-human. As Donna Haraway emphasizes in the first lines of the introduction to *Staying with the Trouble*, "We—all of us on Terra—live in disturbing times, mixed-up times, troubling and turbid times. The task is to become capable, with each other in all of our bumptious kinds, of response."[4]

I believe that the uncertainty of our present is marked by the increasingly evident and simultaneous co-existence of opposed social, historical and ecological forces (such as growth and decay) that shape our time in a series of frictions and tensions. Perhaps we can become capable of response by starting from a deeper emotional understanding of this turbidity and the forces that generate it. In this sense, I believe that artistic language can help us perceive the meshes we are part of, by offering us perspectives and tools with which to experience and express our relation with the transformations of our time as a species and as individuals. Reflecting on the opposition of growth and decay, and on how the distance between the materiality of what appears and the mesh in which it's entangled creates disorientation and friction in our perception of reality, I began working on *Sketches of Transition* by combining opposing and contrasting shapes and materials. Simple geometric elements such as lines and

　　　　　Michele Bazzoli

circles became the basis for more complex forms, shaped into
vertical wooden structures that may recall hypothetical archi-
tectural elements, but which gradually fade into more physical
and visceral references to the body. I developed each sculpture
by layering polyurethane foam and acrylic plaster on wood,
as a hidden reference to how buildings, vehicles and objects are
generally built: by stratification of processes, materials, origins,
and destinations.

We find ourselves in a transition that does not present
itself as a process of overcoming or yet another production
of the new (in avant-garde terms), but rather as a process that
demands a reinterpretation of the past and redefinition of our
present, the paradigm shift of which has not yet been completed.
By looking at how other visual artists attempt to cope with our
present's transformations through the creation of autonomous
visual languages, in particular sculpture, I notice the creation
of symbolism and metaphor, or other figures such as the synec-
doche. These are the cases where the work of an artist is config-
ured as a symbolic translation of the real dynamics of our present,
whose internal logic represents the whole that surrounds it in a
finite portion of space and matter. Furthermore—and I do not
necessarily think of it as a defect—I believe that these metaphor-
ical approaches precisely stem from the clash between the need to
tell about our present and its increasingly complex and elusive
portability into all-encompassing images. In this sense, this clash
often renders symbolic representation more effective.

Could this symbolic dimension provide us a key to deci-
pher and understand our relationship with the contemporary
world and its transformations? Something that makes it difficult
to answer this question is that in the current debate on ecology
and the arts, the very hinges of the system human/art/world are
profoundly changing. Whereas its human production remains
an ontological feature of art, the world today has to be decolo-
nized and is increasingly less anthropocentric. In other words,
the object of artistic production no longer coincides with our
direct relationship to the world as *for us*, but more and more
with the effects of this relationship on the world as it is *for the
world itself*. Starting from this paralyzing asymmetry, art may
finally enter a new symbolic era, of which we are part as much
as the non-human. In this sense, artistic creation does not take
a form from the inside, but it receives it from the outside: it is
not an era in which art aims to express what we are in relation

                    SKETCHES OF TRANSITION

to the world through its own materials, but rather an era in which
art impresses in its materials what the world is *in itself*. As much
as the human intellect remains the ultimate spectator of art,
its anthropocentric view does no longer define any meaningful
horizons against which artistic creation takes place.

Since *Sketches of Transition* developed from the reference to the
plastic tube in La Nada and from my fascination for that place,
I looked for a similar area where to install the work. In The
Netherlands there happens to be several drift-sand areas, and
that of De Loonse en Drunense Duinen (the dunes of Loon and
Drunen) is the largest of Northwest Europe. Not far from
's-Hertogenbosch, where I was studying and working on these
sculptures, it turned out to be a very interesting location where
to set the work and explore the possibility to focus on its ambiguous character by weaving together landscape, sculpture, and
the body, while expanding my research on the role of human
intervention in shaping the land. The area of De Loonse en
Drunense Duinen consists of forests and very large dunes of
shifting sand, creating an extraordinary microclimate, and its
formation arose through the century-long agency of natural
elements combined with human activity. In the last Ice Age,
polar winds blew sand from the north to this region, where
it was deposited in thick layers, later covered with primeval
forests. Until the late Middle Ages, trees were felled for fire-
wood and the area, with its shrublands for grazing, was able to
feed modest farming communities. At that time of relative pros-
perity the population pressure increased to the extent that the
ecosystem was fatally altered by over-grazing and too frequent
plowing of the heath. During the Eighty Years' War the erosion
as a result of agricultural activities was reinforced by exces-
sive deforestation for the production of armament. The sandy
bottom became increasingly exposed, allowing sand to be blown
away by the wind. This process strengthened itself and became
almost unstoppable. Entire medieval villages were buried under
sand. Oak trees were planted to halt desertification, but the
area still declined. Large-scale afforestation, changes in land use,
and nitrogen deposition due to pollution all contributed to the
rapid consolidation of active drift sands. Concurrently, species
related to this specific environment became rare or even went
locally extinct. To maintain this exceptionally large drifting sand
landscape, sand-drift areas have been designated a protected

                    Michele Bazzoli

habitat and efforts are now made to conserve the last remaining areas, or restore the consolidated drift-sand by removing all vegetation and topsoil, and clear surrounding forests to increase erodibility. This environment's conditions have always been deeply shaped by the agency of different factors, including human activities. Future development of the current drift-sand areas or their successful restoration depends on the combination of those external factors that are driving these ecosystems: climate, landscape erodibility and land use. Another important factor is aeolian activity: sediment transport and erosion produced by the wind are constantly transforming the area. Unique tools have been developed to monitor the dynamics of these transformations. For example, dendrogeomorphology is a tool used to reconstruct and study the aeolian activity of these areas in retrospect, read from the structures of the trees. Because signs of past deposition and erosion events are conserved in wood, this is the only method for the reconstruction of drift-sand dynamics when the landforms are no longer present. Oaks, pines, and birch trees frequently establish themselves in drift-sand areas. Oaks occur as single trees or are clustered in groups. Oak clusters originate from oak shrubs or trees that were partially covered by drift sand. DNA analysis demonstrated that oak clusters consist of a single or a few different genotypes forming one or more clones.

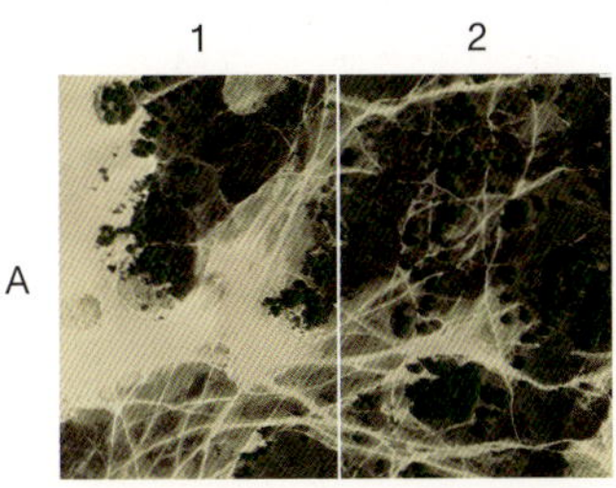

MiB.07　De Loonse en Drunense Duinen, Drunen, The Netherlands, Google Earth view

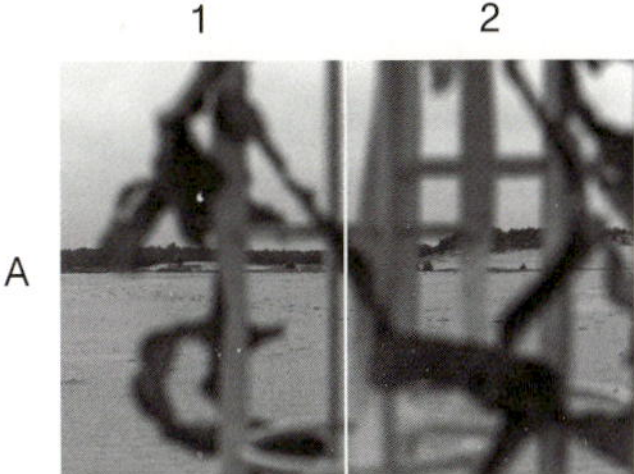

MiB.08　De Loonse en Drunense Duinen, Drunen, The Netherlands, 2020

Creating a parallel with the formation of oak trees and clusters in the dunes, the ten elements that comprise the sculptural installation *Sketches of Transition* have developed from one another, as if forming a cluster in a process of cell mitosis, as if they share the same genome. By shaping each sheet of wood through laser cutting (as in an industrial process), the remaining cut-out parts became the basis for composing other elements, generating clones from their complementary shapes. The simple perpendicular

joints that fix the different parts, bringing the circles and vertical
silhouettes together, are visible when not covered by the foam and
plaster shapes, which are portrayed as developing onto the wood
surfaces or as retracting in themselves. They develop between the
micro and the macro, as if they are scale models for larger construc-
tions or as if they are enlargements of tiny siliceous skeletons of
organisms such as radiolarians. In this 'scalelessness' they are
proportionate to the body, or rather in a one to one relation with
it: they are something which can become a measurement tool
and which (while varying in dimensions) remains an object or
structure with which I could hypothetically interact.

Taking the form of a multitude of carved pillars on which
xenomorph shapes appear in a state of suspended transition
between growth and decay, the installation depicts the hypothetical remains of a crumbling architecture and at the same
time stages elements which have yet to be put into operation
or completed. Led by the desire to participate physically in the
work I was making and in an attempt to further expand its ambi-
guity (the state of in-betweenness where formal references and
different visual remembrances are interwoven), I tried to add a
new element to the installation. I wasn't really looking for an
additional outer layer, but something that would branch, grow
and disintegrate aside, above and inside each of the sculptures.
So I took some of my old working clothes, including a pair of
jeans that I have been wearing while working on the installation.
I tore them along the edges trying to reduce the surface as
much as possible, in an attempt to reach the limit of their state
as garment, almost completely disintegrated and reduced to
lines, so that I could model and arrange the structures of each
element as if they were drawings, adding more lines to *Sketches
of Transition*.

This gesture was a first attempt to formalize a reflection
on the odd alterity of matter, which sometimes feels normal and
at other times uncanny. Our garments are probably the closest
objects to our bodies and the material with which we intimately
interact the most. When we discard instead of recycle them, they
decompose and cease to fit the body, gradually becoming part of
something else. Just like dead skin gets detached from our body
and dispersed around us imperceptibly, every object that defines
our surrounding material reality decays, spreading traces of
our physical existence everywhere. In this sense, the presence
of these useless garments within the wooden structures of the

 Michele Bazzoli

installation evokes the presence and physicality of the phantasmatic 'elsewhere' (the ideal destination of our waste). In fact, this 'place' corresponds to an increasingly concrete dimension which is part of our environment and which urgently demands our attention. Upon completion, all the elements of *Sketches of Transition* were temporarily installed in the drift-sand area of De Loonse en Drunense Duinen, for the time needed to document them. The work appears as a set of elements, foreign to that environment while also wanting to belong there—like the plastic fragments in the photos from La Nada. Avoiding direct representation, each is formed as a self-standing sculpture that seems to have absorbed its pedestal. *Sketches of Transition* wants to offer an image in which different dimensions and temporalities coexist, and also reflect on the character of our troubled and restless times. The visual documentation of the installation in this unique environment is the final stage of the work and has been made especially for this publication.

1   George Bataille, *The Labyrinth, The Labyrinth in Vision Of Excesses. Selected Writings*, 1927 – 1939, University of Minnesota Press, Minneapolis, 1985, p.173

2   Graham Harman, *Object-oriented-ontology. A New Theory of Everything*, Penguin Books, London, 2018, p.73

3   Timothy Morton, *Hyperobjects. Philosophy and Ecology after the End of the World*, University of Minnesota Press, Minneapolis, 2013, p.49

4   Donna Haraway, *Staying with the trouble – Making Kin in the Chtulhucene*, Duke University Press, Durham and London, 2016, p.1

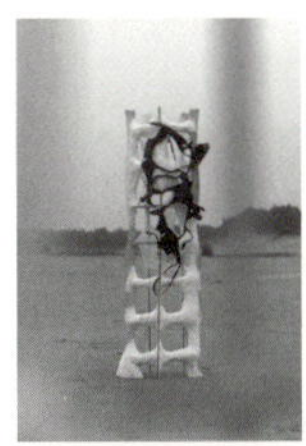

MiB.09   *Sketches of Transition*, 2021, wood, foam, glass fiber, plasticrete, sand, sawdust, plaster, fabric, installation view in De Loonse en Drunense Duinen, photo by Hussel Zhu

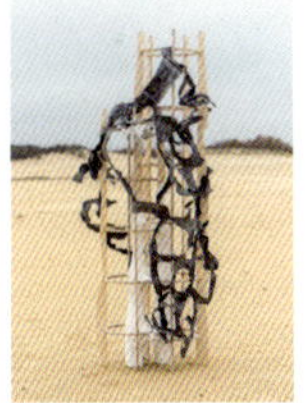

MiB.10   Idem.

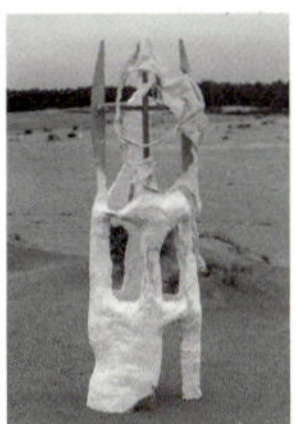

MiB.11   Idem.

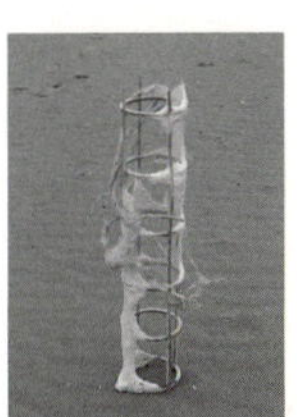

MiB.12   *Sketches of Transition*, 2021, De Loonse en Drunense Duinen, photo by Michele Bazzoli, 2021

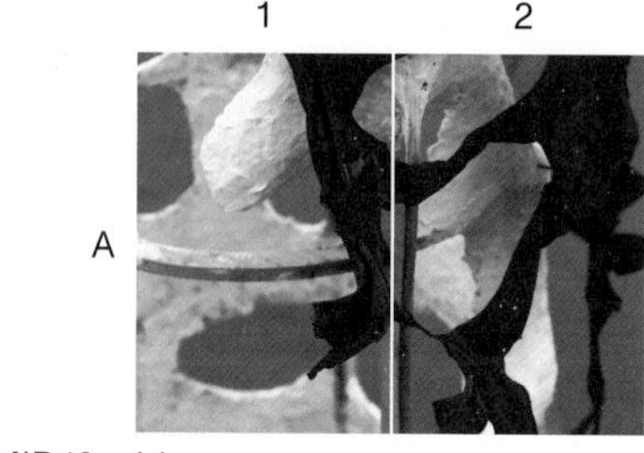

MiB.13   Idem.

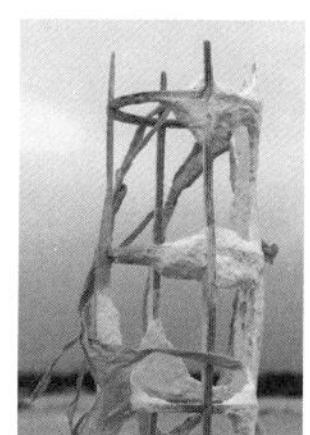

MiB.14   Idem.

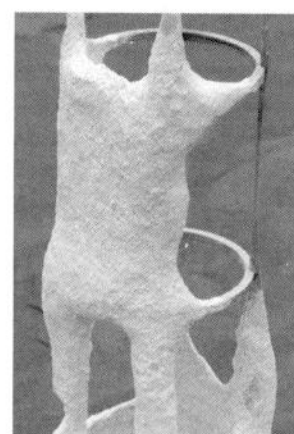

MiB.15   Idem.

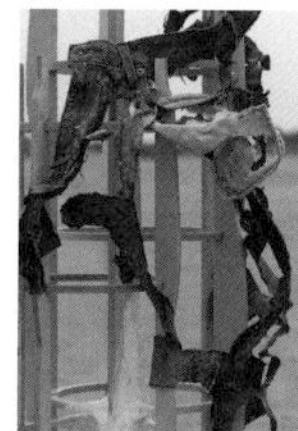

MiB.16   Idem.

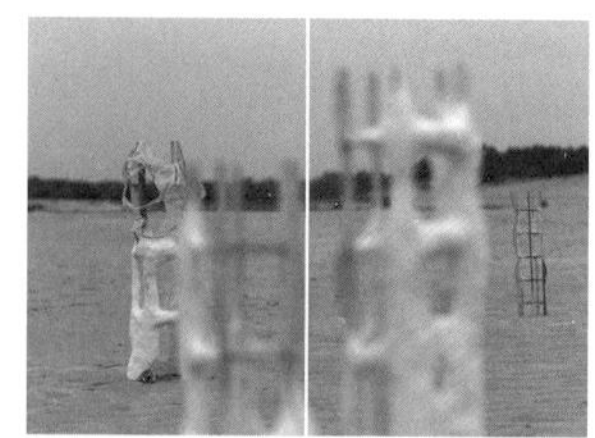

MiB.17   *Sketches of Transition*, 2021,
De Loonse en Drunense Duinen,
photo by Hussel Zhu

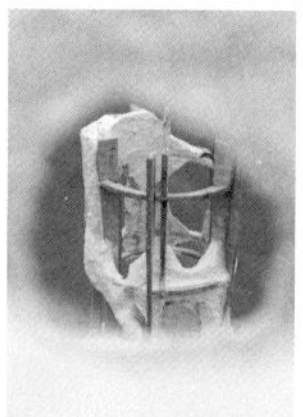

MiB.18   Idem.

Michele Bazzoli

Dagmar Bosma

DREDGING

My first ever visit to Brienenoord island in Rotterdam was in
the spring of 2020. There's a path that circumvents the island,
but when you leave the path you can go down to the edges of
the island, to its sandy banks, and at low tide you can find lots of
stuff naked and uncovered on the beach. That's where you can
find things that have sort of merged, weathered industrial ruins
and remnants of human activity that have been overgrown to the
point of being almost indistinguishable from the 'wild' nature
of the island. You probably wouldn't notice these things at first.

I started gleaning during the first months of lockdown as
a way to find something to hold onto. On Brienenoord's beaches
I found pieces of scrap metal, which are easy to overlook because
they've rusted to the point where their surface has become
porous and flaky. Their exterior is bursting, expanding. That's
the strange thing about rust, as you would assume an object to
become smaller instead of bigger, while it withers in the process
of erosion. But rust actually expands, layering out like puff pastry
and flaking off at the same time. Every time I pick up or move a
rusted object a bit of shedding happens. I always find tiny particles of rust at the bottom of the bag in which I carry my gleaned
metal. The scraps look like chunks of bark. When your eyes have
become more familiarized, you will be able to recognize the
rusted objects and not mistake them for branches or twigs. But
sometimes you would still pick up what you think is a piece of
scrap metal, which then turns out to be a piece of wood. You'll
know for sure that something's made of metal when you lift it up
and feel its weight as well as the slight coldness and roughness
of its surface. Dragging around heavy metal helped me to regain
a sensory understanding of the weight of things around me, which,
contrary to what my bodily instincts were telling me all the time,
would not float away to dissolve into thin air.

Pipelines and thick metal wires stick out from the island's
banks. Its rubble beaches are littered with broken tiles and
complete concrete footers and kitchen sinks. The pipes and wires
seem to be keeping all the rubble together. Down at the beach
you will find the naked roots of trees, like mangroves, where
many things have become entangled with the root network.
Tree roots have grown all around the bricks perched in between

131

them. Then there are bundled textiles, torn scarves and T-shirts wrapped around trees in a way you would not be able to untie them. The coming-together of things here is sculptural. These are wild sculptures. A sort of synthetic wool has felted together with the moss. Because they have grown into each other they can no longer be separated. There are more recent arrivals, too: beer cans, tiny decorative flags used for some kind of outdoor parties, and condoms.

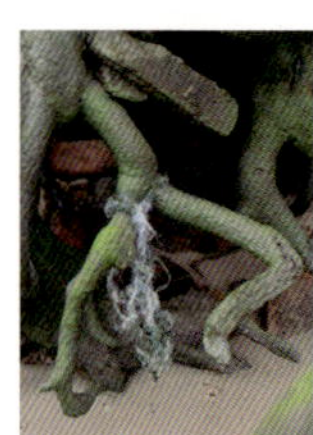

DB.01   Wild sculpture at Brienenoord island, photo by Dagmar's grandfather Onno Bosma

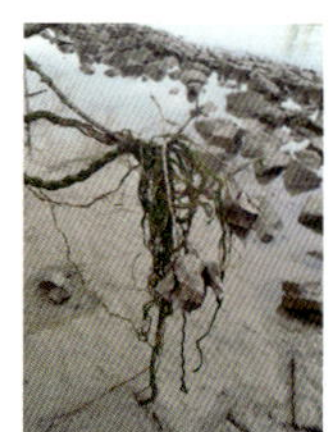

DB.02   Idem.

What can be observed at Brienenoord's rubble beaches is an ongoing process of co-authored making between natural forces and the residue of things washed ashore. As if nature doesn't mind the rubble and just absorbs it. In the co-creation of wild sculptures, things constantly seep into each other and change their shape through the closeness of other presences and processes. One has a rough awakening from fantasies about nature's original pristinity when exploring murky wastelands like Brienenoord, a wild place that is all about filth and decay.

Brienenoord island began to emerge in the early nineteenth century after a long process of siltation: the building up of clay particles on waterbeds caused by land erosion. Siltation is understood as a type of water pollution, as the 'increased accumulation (temporary or permanent) of sediments on bottoms where they are undesirable.' Through the growth of reeds and other vegetation, patches of layered silt became connected so to form a larger surface. These shallow muddy grounds gained more body after World War II, when rubble from Rotterdam's bombed city center was buried there to form a more elevated island. Apparently entire church buildings rest in pieces on its banks. It's safe to state that Brienenoord came into being through spoiled formation—the thickening of residue.

After World War II the island was mostly home to recreational clubhouses and some small industries. In the 1960s tunnel elements for the Rotterdam metro were built on a dock specifically

                     Dagmar Bosma

designed for this purpose. After an intense industrial period, the Rotterdam municipality gained ownership over the island and began to treat it as a sort of wasteland, an undeveloped 'empty' space, left bare and waiting to be filled between periods of construction or after demolition. This supposed emptiness triggered an itch and was met with an urge for urban development: in the past half century Brienenoord has been the imagined destination for a plethora of wild plans. Such plans included standard building like real estate and hotels, but in the 1970s a proposal was made to erect an 'eros center', which would concentrate the many streetwalking sex workers of the Katendrecht area in a centralized high-rise brothel. These plans met with local resistance or lacked the financial backing to be realized.

Currently, a tidal ecosystem is being developed on the island: it's the first of many wild plans actually being put in motion. Work has started to transform Brienenoord's surface and landscape, a transformation that is realized mainly through dredging, which clears the river bedding through the scooping out of mud, vegetation and rubbish with a dredge. Parts of the banks are dug out to form lagoons, after which the remaining mud will be dumped at the tips of the island to increase its surface area. The island's haphazardly formed banks are smoothened so they will be more welcoming for certain plant species and wildlife. In addition, the island is reshaped to be more accessible to Rotterdam's population through the construction of a new entrance bridge and lookout points and platforms. Some locals have meanwhile voiced their concerns and think their beloved wild island will become too *clean*.

From the perspective of normative human activity (the dominant perspective in urban development, even when it comes to so-called natural areas like Brienenoord), 'nothing' happens in the wasteland. Contrary to such readings, the pre-developed state of Brienenoord island offers a decentralized space for queer encounters between different matters and species. Half man-made and half wild, the island serves as a refuge for washed-up things and beings to encounter and merge. It is in this place without destination where they find an arena to meet. In places of not-one-thing-in-particular a multitude of particularities can roam. Nothingness, in the words of theoretical physicist and feminist theorist Karen Barad, is the 'scene of wild activities'.

   DREDGING

When we consider Brienenoord's status as a popular spot for cruising and other wayward sexual activities, the current developments and earlier plans are of a complex significance. Whereas an eros center was meant to keep loitering sex workers off the slum streets, now the instalment of a hyper visible landscape of vistas and lookout points will surely scare away those who came to the island to cruise. Both are instances of the centralization of sex. Both the wasteland and the sexual activities it harbors have to be gathered around a center, developed towards a destination of perceived purity.

If the island were to remain wild it should at least be really, really wild, to stand as an example of nature's unmitigated splendor and functioning. No more post-industrial ruins and jizz-filled condoms! Why allowing exhibitionist homosexuals or Polish immigrant workers to frequent the island to fish and fuck and party and leave behind beer cans and rubbers, when instead you can attract The Genuine Nature-lover, The Yuppy Family, The Young Creative on a Latte Break? Paradoxically the eco-sanitization of Brienenoord is organized with the aim to make wildness flourish, but mainly for that wildness to be put on display and facilitate normative human-centric activities. Here wildness is made accessible, so that some will stay away.

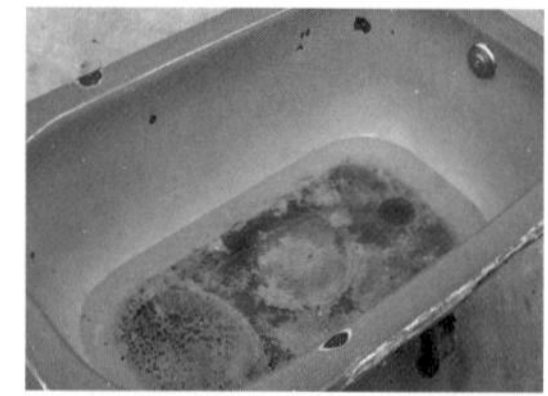

DB.03   *Scrap Metal Dream Boy* (detail), 2021, bathtub, lubricant

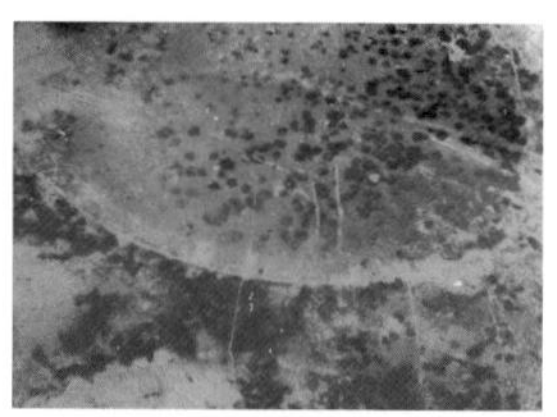

DB.04   *Scrap Metal Dream Boy* (detail), 2021, bathtub, lubricant

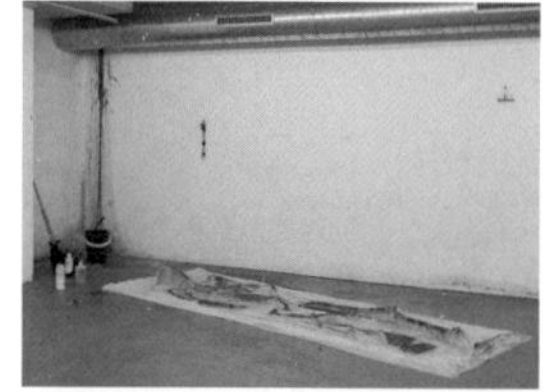

DB.05   *Scrap Metal Dream Boy* (installation view), 2021, scrap metal, rust-dyed fabric, in-situ cleaning supplies

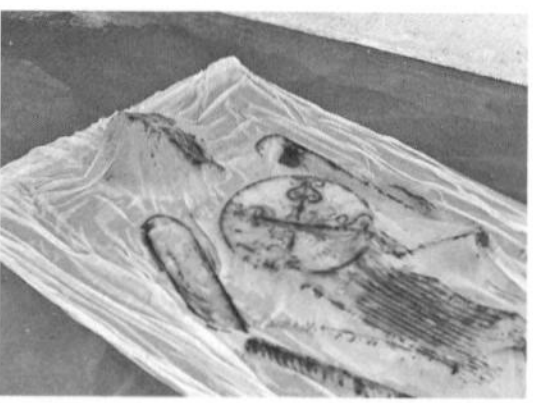

DB.06   *Scrap Metal Dream Boy* (detail), 2021, scrap metal, rust-dyed fabric, in-situ cleaning supplies

          Dagmar Bosma

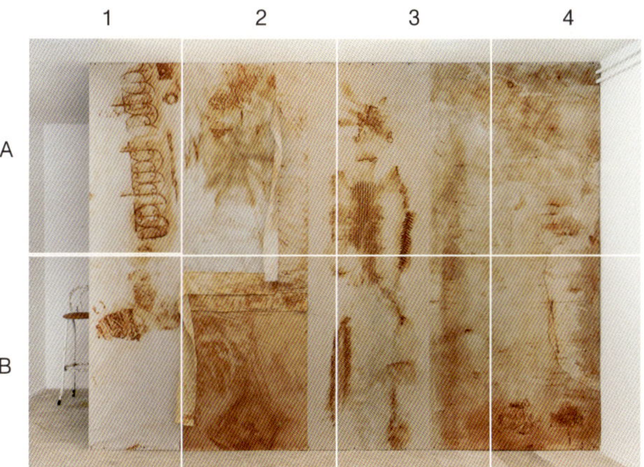

DB.07   *Scrap Metal Dream Boy*, 2021, rust-dyed fabric

Scrap Metal Dream Boy is a body of work that started to form while gleaning for metal remnants around Brienenoord and other post-industrial wastelands in Rotterdam. Loosely assembled and trans*ferred onto fabric with rust-dyeing techniques, these seemingly exhausted bits and pieces come alive as auratic entities. Unproductive queer potentialities are found in the worn-out: in that which is no longer able to function as it should.

The work follows the trans*itory entropic movement of oxidation and corrosion, in which material passionately drives towards its own erosive undoing. Iron only becomes chemically stable when it rusts and flakes beyond repair. Shapeshifting and spreading tenaciously, rust makes brittle what was once impermeable.

     DREDGING

Lara Almarcegui

GRAVES
Max Andrews & Mariana Cánepa Luna

Juxtaposing two new projects, Lara Almarcegui's Graves (Gravels) is a work that offers a geological perspective on the Lleida area, and the floodplain of the Segre, through the relationship between the built environment and the vast mountain belt that formed between 80 and 20 million years ago as the Iberian Peninsula crashed into the rest of Europe – the Pyrenees.

Described in the most succinct way, the first project is a response to the question: What quantities of which rocks and materials constitute the Pyrenees? Arriving at the answer has involved collaborating with geologists on a complex series of clarifications, calculations, and 3D modelling. Where do the Pyrenees begin and end? What level of detail is desirable? It results in Rocas y Materiales de la Cordillera de los Pirineos (2021), an austere ordered list, presented at La Panera as a large wall text.

The second asks: What possibilities begin to emerge when the excavation at a quarry is stopped? More specifically, when La Plana del Corb, the industrial complex operated by Sorigué near the town of Balaguer, temporarily stops its operations for a single day? The response takes the form of an open day at the quarry on 19 February 2021 in which visitors experience this otherwise usually bustling and noisy place as a site of contemplation. At La Panera, Gravera (2021), a large video projection at the opposite end of the space from the list of materials, presents documentation of the same stopped quarry standing still in time. With no droning machinery, hissing water jets, or crunching and mounding gravel, we witness a stark granular landscape of artificial cliffs, islands, and isthmuses of terrain, from which the long necks of conveyor belts emerge, frozen as if mechanical dinosaurs. In between these two new projects by Almarcegui, the onerous chasm of the stone-walled art centre suggests a stratigraphic imaginary replete with the slow violence of the Earth's morphological transformation and the contrastingly temporary nature of manmade construction.

As the monographic title indicates, Almarcegui brings to the surface a form of geopoetics, geophilosophy, and geohistory that centres on gravel, a loose conglomeration of rock fragments, a not-yet sand.

137

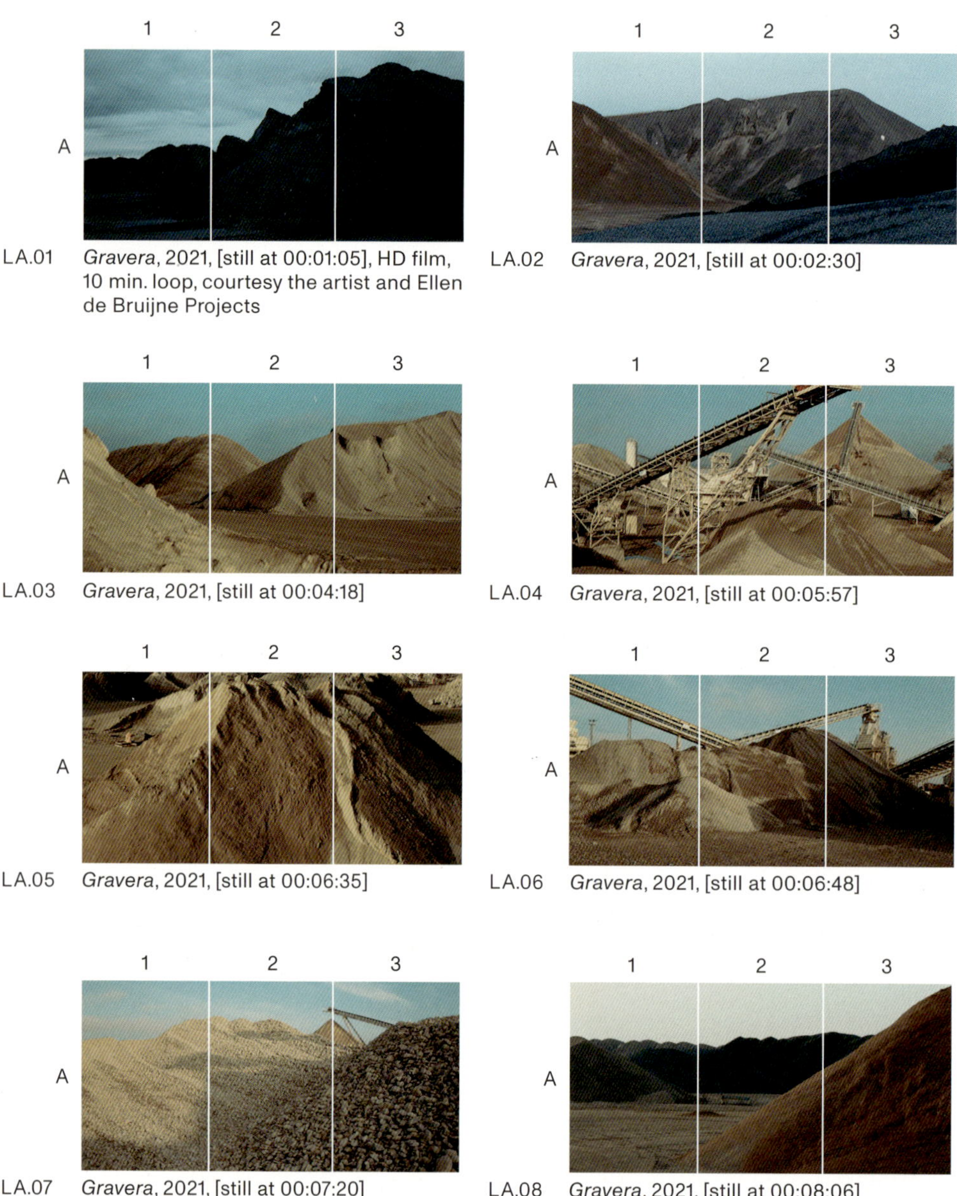

LA.01   *Gravera*, 2021, [still at 00:01:05], HD film,
10 min. loop, courtesy the artist and Ellen
de Bruijne Projects

LA.02   *Gravera*, 2021, [still at 00:02:30]

LA.03   *Gravera*, 2021, [still at 00:04:18]

LA.04   *Gravera*, 2021, [still at 00:05:57]

LA.05   *Gravera*, 2021, [still at 00:06:35]

LA.06   *Gravera*, 2021, [still at 00:06:48]

LA.07   *Gravera*, 2021, [still at 00:07:20]

LA.08   *Gravera*, 2021, [still at 00:08:06]

Different grades of gravel have been extracted from La Plana del
Corb over the last 25 years. Once sorted and processed, the gravels
and grits are predominately destined for use in concrete and asphalt,
in addition to other manmade deposits such as embankment fills,
foundations, drainage beds, and playgrounds. These diverse miscel-
lanies of small stones and mineral debris are eroded and displaced
mountains, an abiding disaggregation of the Pyrenees. Matter that
has been removed from the planes for little more than two decades
moved down to the lowlands like lithic glaciers over a length of time
on a human scale that may as well be forever. Once gouged by ice and

                         Lara Almarcegui

flushed out of the mountains by turbulent streams rushing through the ancient pinnacles and foothills, it travelled in floods, thickened primal river beds, filled valleys – spreading wide and washing out into deep deposits and deltas. Quartzes, slates, and hornfels; schists, limestones, and granites: picking through the gravel is like sorting evidence from a primordial explosion. Looking from Almarcegui's documentary video to the mountains in list form we read across and upwards from one world to another. From future buildings and infrastructure to the ancient natural formations that their components once came from.

Almarcegui has produced a whole series of such geological inventories, compiling the volume or mass of the principal 'ingredients' of single museum buildings, entire urban areas such as São Paulo, and landmasses, including the island of Spitsbergen. These rock taxonomies and construction ledgers present both stark statements of apparent material facts, and exercises of reckoning that describe how modernity was founded on the abstraction and illusion of the Earth as a resource.

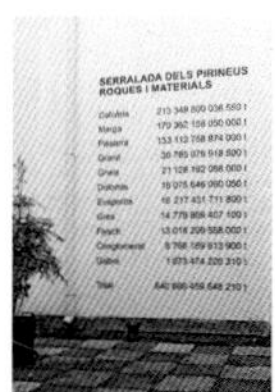

LA.09   *Rocks and materials of the Pyrenees mountains range*, 2021, dimensions variable, courtesy the artist and Ellen de Bruijne Projects, photo by Jeroen de Smalen

Through the somewhat implausible exercise of measuring a mountain range, Almarcegui broaches the paradox that the practices of standardisation, quantification, and mathematisation that have given rise to extraordinary value and knowledge over the last centuries, also represent the progression of a perspective that has allowed the commodification and management of nature. The globe was reimagined through mapping, measuring, and surveying during the 18th and 19th centuries. Such revolutionary metrical processes accelerated the appropriation of nature's wealth, bringing it under systematic control and facilitating its capitalisation. Geology was crucial to this externalising of nature and the economising of the world. As it deepened as a field of knowledge during the 1800s, it allowed nature to be dismissed as something immobile, impassive, and immense – so much so that the Earth's

                    GRAVES

limits then seemed invisible. The first geological maps, developed by English geologist William Smith, were innovations that also allowed mining to become more predictable and cost-effective. The realisation that the Earth was inordinately older than the 6,000 year age that could be derived from the Bible re-calibrated nature as something vast and slow, rather than capricious and catastrophic. The abundant endowment evoked by this longer-and-deeper perspective ensured that the planet could be more easily imagined as an inexhaustible reserve. By the late 19th century, concerns about the depletion of the mineral world had been overcome by the establishment of the notion of global resources. The narrative of the Earth became desensitised to human actions and social phenomena. Disciplines diverged into the study of human history on the one hand, and natural science on the other. A wall arose between the time of man and the time of nature, between the tiny sliver of time comprising human history and the vast geological timescale of the planet.

Almarcegui's work attempts nothing less than a convergence of these broken timeframes through the force of art and a tacking back-and-forth of scales and temporalities between gravel and buildings, the apparent 'stopped clock' of extraction during a single day, and the sheer mass of a 'timeless' millions-of-years-old mountain belt. Both the industry of La Plana del Corb, and the industry involved in calculating the mass of the Pyrenees, seek to extract value and somehow compute phenomena that are, in important senses, immeasurable and unexplainable, and that far exceed the illusions that we have sufficient knowledge. The exhibition Graves produces a mountain range in the human imagination, a mountain range that is also the constructed world in our here and now. And what appears at first to be a purely quantitive reflection on materials and measurements is instead both poetic and shocking: the cliff-edge of our own ignorance.

          Lara Almarcegui

Yana Naidenov

QUANTUM HAUNTOLOGIES

The printed works featured in this publication consist of eclectic montages digitally printed on textile, which include sculpted wire drawings, photographs of ropes placed randomly over bleached fabric, images sourced from a personal archive, as well diagrams of molecular models and knots sourced from the internet. The technique of sublimation allows for varying degrees of transparency seen through the fabric and, along with the visual elements, there are multiple overlaps in the visual compositions which evoke a sense of enmeshment and spectrality. I became aware of a space – or rather a kind of non-place – that these digital structures began to occupy in the image field; a type of interior virtual space.

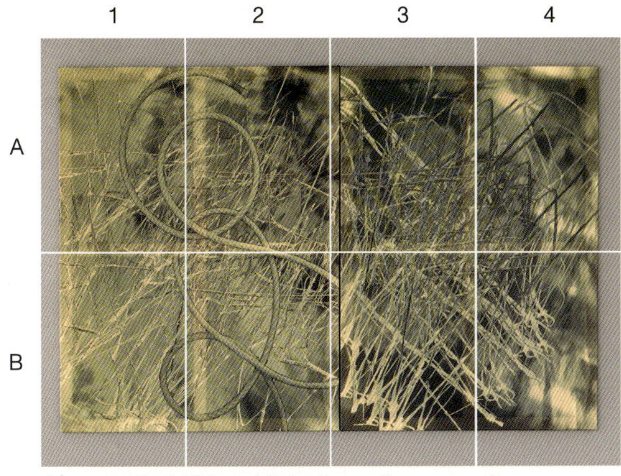

YN.01   *Ghost web*, 2022, sublimation print on textile,
90 × 125cm and 98 × 125cm

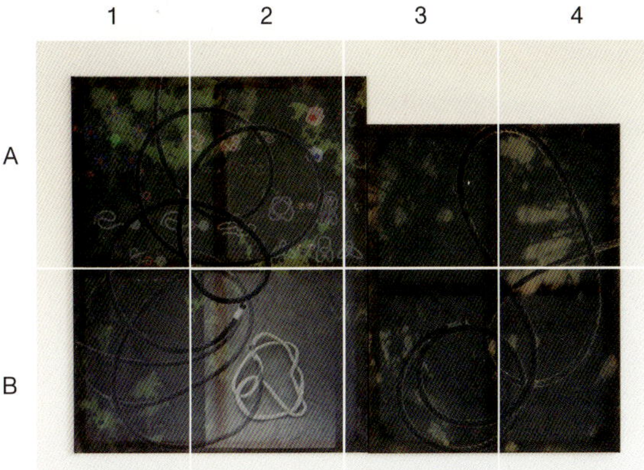

YN.02   *X-ray crystal structure of a molecular pentafoil
knot*, 2022, sublimation print on textile, 145 × 115cm
and 98 × 125cm

I began working on these montages in a way that I like to describe as automatic, similarly to automatic writing, where you write without concern for sentence structure nor meaning, from a place that is both pre- and post-linguistic – as a means of articulating into the conscious what lies in the subconscious. This process of working may be best described as a state of mind, perhaps, an overriding of the rational with an exploratory, aimless disposition, where I'm really just putting my mind to one side and going for a more process-oriented, "seeing-what-happens" kind of making. Automatic writing is also referred to as *psychography*, and that's interesting for me because the images seem to allude to a place in the psyche rather than a physical or external place.

I started with a very simple, almost dumb process of repeatedly throwing a rope in the air and recording photographically how it randomly fell on the ground, each time observing how it never landed in the same place nor with the same configuration. This *automatic* method of working became quite close to that of drawing, in the sense that you go from one step to the next as though you were making a line of procedures. I then transposed the images onto the screen, edited and modified them. To me these ropes serve as a vocabulary of displacement – they lack structure, they can be dispersed and stretched over space; they are centreless and rhizomatic. However I was also drawn to an apparent primitiveness of their shape, reminiscent of snakes. Seeing coiled, serpentine forms on the ground seems to evoke a primordial reptilian memory of some kind. This seemed congruent with the subconscious dimension that this automatic process, as mentioned before, seems to draw from.

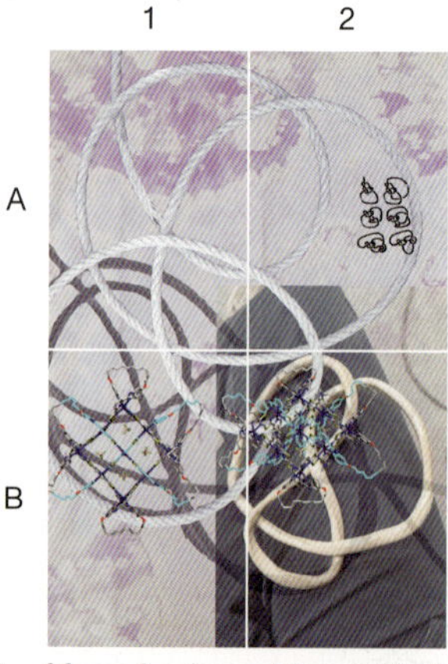

YN.03 *Many-body problems*, 2022,
sublimation print on textile,
145 × 115 cm

                    Yana Naidenov

The post-conceptual artist Seth Price's series *Knot Paintings* features skins of plastic with a hollow vacuum-formed shape at the centre, where a semi-coiled rope used to be (the title is a word play on 'not-paintings'). I've always been drawn to these works because they don't seem to belong anywhere – they're neither painting nor sculpture, neither abstract nor figurative – they're mechanically aided, yet sequentially handmade. They appear to be at this crux between art, new media and the ready-made, which characterizes the sense of displacement in Price's work, and that's something I really identify with. Introducing new media into the production and circulation of artworks changes the art instrument into something that is difficult to categorize due to the state of liminality it comes to occupy.

In the case of the printed works, physical objects have been displaced onto the digital and reproduced back into the physical, yet they are now these flattened hollow spectres of what used to be. Working with digital material is to me like operating in the realm of ghosts, of things that aren't there. This may seem like an antithesis to the three-dimensional, yet this paradoxical zone where the intangibility of the digital (akin to the psychic) exchanges with the physical has always been a point of fascination for me, as it sits alongside a very primary impulse of making cultural objects or images as a means of communicating or channelling something latent or noumenal.

The analogy of the ghost becomes useful when negotiating these contradictions, these liminal states between two things. It's a state that appears to be increasingly the *modus operandi* of contemporaneity, of being present physically and digitally at the same time – and so it seems that much of our psychic space is transposed, or occupied by the digital. In a sense it has become the norm to constantly migrate between these states, and for this reason I think humans have come to occupy a place of ghostliness, of being two (or at least more than one), where these presences and absences and constantly negotiated. Jacques Derrida had a pretty good term for this – hauntology, or *hantologie* – that is a "haunted" "ontology", a "being ghost", where he ascribes a corporeal function to the spectral (particularly as it is evoked through the mediations of new technologies). In *Spectres of Marx* (1994), Derrida states that '[f]or there to be a ghost, there must be a return to the body, but to a body that is more abstract than ever. The spectrogenic process corresponds to a paradoxical incorporation', proposing that

the ghost re-emerges as the "more than one/no more one [*le plus d'un*]"[1] in hauntology. This has helped me articulate what in my work feels like is an ongoing a process of materializing ghosts.

1   Jacques Derrida, *Specters of Marx*, Routledge, 1993, p.157

    Yana Naidenov

LARA ALMARCEGUI (Zaragoza, 1972) lives and works in Rotterdam. Her work has been the object of numerous solo exhibitions in institutions such as Graphische Sammlung, Zurich (2019); IVAM, Valencia, Spain (2019); Art Basel (2018); Casino Luxembourg (2016); Kunsthaus Baselland, Switzerland (2015); Gemeente Museum Den Haag, the Netherlands (2015); the Stedelijk Museum, Den Bosch (2012). Almarcegui has also participated in many collective exhibitions in institutions such as Kröller-Müller Museum, Otterlo (2020), Centro Botín, Santander (2020), Kunsthalle Karlsruhe (2020), Museum M+, Hong Kong (2019), MACBA, Barcelona (2015), and Van Abbemuseum, Eindhoven (2015), among others. Almarcegui has also participated in the 14th Biennale de Lyon, France (2017); the 1st Triennale of Aichi, Nagoya, Japan (2013); Manifesta 9 (2012); the Taipei Biennial (2010); the 2nd Athens Biennial (2011). In 2013 she represented Spain at the 55th Venice Biennale.

MARIA BARNAS (Hoorn, 1973) is a writer, poet and visual artist. Barnas studied at the Rietveld Academie and the Rijksakademie in Amsterdam (1998-2000). Since her poetry debut with Twee Zonnen in 2003, for which she was given the C. Buddingh'-prijs in 2004, she has been awarded numerous prizes including the Ger Fritz-Prijs (2021); Leo Herberghs Poëzieprijs (2016); Anna Bijns Prijs (2014), among others. Her work is represented by Galerie Annet Gelink, Amsterdam, and was showcased in several solo exhibitions in museums as Kröller-Müller museum, Otterlo (2019); Nationaal Glasmuseum, Leerdam (2017); Museum De Hallen, Haarlem (2016), among others.

In 2016 she was nominated member of the Akademie van Kunsten; and in 2022 she was nominated City Poet by the municipality of Alkmaar. Barnas also published three novels, Engelen van ijs (1997), De baadster (2000), and Altijd Augustus (2017).

MICHELE BAZZOLI (Brescia, 1996) is an Italian visual artist based in Amsterdam, the Netherlands. After completing a bachelor's degree in Painting at the Brera Academy of Fine Arts in Milan, Italy, he attained a master's degree in Visual Arts & Ecology Futures at the Master Institute of Visual Cultures in 's-Hertogenbosch, the Netherlands. His work was presented in solo and group exhibitions at Galleria Lampo, Milan (2023); Het Blauwe Veld, Arnhem (2022); Zaza Ramen, Milan (2022); Galleria Arrivada, Milan (2021); DOOR, Dordrecht (2021); SK Galerie, Solingen (2021); 9hrs Capsule Hotel, Tokyo (2019). In 2023 he is selected for the ARTeCHÓ fellowship program, and his work has been included in the catalogue 99 Future Blue-Chip Artists by Artsted.

DAGMAR BOSMA (The Hague, 1994) is an artist, writer and gleaner based in Rotterdam, the Netherlands. They obtained a master's degree in Fine Art at the Piet Zwart Institute in Rotterdam (2021), and a bachelor's degree in Philosophy at the University of Amsterdam (2018).Bosma's work has recently been shown in solo and group exhibitions at A Tale of A Tub, Rotterdam (2023), Kunstfort Vijfhuizen, Vijfhuizen (2023), Flippy's, Melbourne (2023), Rosa Kwir, Balzan (2023), Dracul.la, L'Hospitalet de Llobregat (2022), and Available and the Rat, Rotterdam (2021). Their texts and essays have been published by several magazines and online platforms, including Metropolis M, Mister Motley, zweikommasieben, and Tubelight. Currently, they are an editor at Girls Like Us magazine and nY magazine. From 2016 to 2020 they have been part of the curatorial team at Stichting Perdu, a centre for poetry and experiment in Amsterdam.

YANA NAIDENOV (Maputo, 1988) completed a BA in Interaction Design (2010) at the London College of Communication, and a Master's in Sculpture at the Royal College of Art (2013), London, UK. Between 2016 and 2018 she was resident at De Ateliers in Amsterdam, Netherlands. Since 2010 she has exhibited internationally, with solo exhibitions at Artes - Mota Galiza (2022, Porto, Portugal), De Ateliers (2018, Amsterdam, Netherlands), CASS Sculpture Foundation (2016, Chichester, UK), Josh Lilley (2015, London, UK); and group exhibitions at Museum Jan (2022, Amstelveen Netherlands), Tatjana Pieters (2021, Gent, Belgium), Institut für Bienenzucht (2017, London, UK), Artíssima (2016, Turin, Italy), 53 Beck Road (2015, London, UK), Leila Heller (2014, New York, USA), and Yorkshire Sculpture Park (2013, Wakefield, UK).

In 2020, she participated in Al Balad's virtual residency, hosted by ATHR Gallery, Saudi Arabia. She was a resident artist at the EKWC (European Ceramic Workcenter) Oisterwijk, in 2021, with support from the Calouste Gulbenkian Foundation. In 2022 she was selected for the Topographic Atlas commission, by the Municipality of Amstelveen, Netherlands.

ACKNOWLEDGMENTS

The reasons why I began the journey that led to the publishing of this book were rather simple: after my studies at the Master Institute of Visual Cultures in 's-Hertogenbosch I wished to further develop my thesis *On Growth and Decay—Amidst the Transition*. Due to time limitations and some academic regulations it became a relatively short paper. Besides, I wanted to document the related sculptural installation *Sketches of Transition* in an outside location. Only after bringing together an initial version of the text and some pictures of the installation situated in the sand-drift area De Loonse en Drunense Duinen, I began to sense that the book could become a platform where to host and support some practices and researches alongside mine.

I want to thank all the participating artists, whose work I admire and deeply fascinates me, for their trust and contributions. Many thanks to Kai Udema, who carefully designed the book and structured its architecture into an atlas with an innovative way to navigate it.

I also wish to thank the people involved with the different contributions: Dr. Francisco Javier Serón Torrecilla from the Escuela Superior de Diseño de Aragón and Dr. Óscar Pueyo Anchuela from the University of Zaragoza for their availability and precious information around the geomorphology of Cuarte de Huerva; Ellen de Bruijne Projects in Amsterdam for their courtesy in providing visual documentation of Lara Almarcegui's work; and to the curatorial office Latitudes in Barcelona for letting me include their wonderful text produced on the occasion of Almarcegui's exhibition at La Panera Art Centre.

Thanks to Franka van de Goor of Atelier Beheer Stichting, and to artist Shirley Welten for hosting me during a writing residency at Nova Zembla, where I began to shape the outline for this book.

Thanks to gallerist Mieke van Schaijk for her help and advice.

Thanks to my former tutors and artists Philippine Hoegen and Rosie Heinrich for their advice and to Mariska van den Berg for her dedication and tutoring during the writing of my master's thesis. Thanks to fellow artists and friends Hussel Zhu and Robert Lombarts for their help in documenting *Sketches of Transition* in De Loonse en Drunense Duinen; and to everyone who more or less directly contributed to this project. Special thanks to Elisabetta Roselli, for her support, help, and love.

The realization of this book has been made possible by the generous support of Gemeente 's-Hertogenbosch Cultuurfondsen, Jaap Harten Fonds, Mondriaan Fund, and Onomatopee.

Michele Bazzoli

SKETCHES OF TRANSITION
An Atlas on Growth and Decay

Lara Almarcegui
Maria Barnas
Michele Bazzoli
Dagmar Bosma
Yana Naidenov

Onomatopee 246

Curation and editing
Michele Bazzoli

Design and concept
Kai Udema

Texts by
Maria Barnas
Michele Bazzoli
Dagmar Bosma
Yana Naidenov

'Graves' was written by Latitudes (Max Andrews &
Mariana Cánepa Luna), commissioned by the Centre
d'art La Panera in Lleida and published on the occasion
of Lara Almarcegui's exhibition *Graves* curated by
Cèlia del Diego, February – May 2021.

Proofreading and text editing
Taco Hidde Bakker

Printing
Drukkerij Tielen

Binding
Boekbinderij Patist

Publisher
Onomatopee Projects, Eindhoven NL
Jesse Muller and Natasha Rijkhoff

Financial support by
Gemeente 's-Hertogenbosch Cultuurfondsen
Jaap Harten Fonds
Mondriaan Fonds
Onomatopee

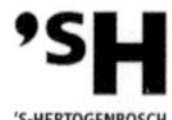 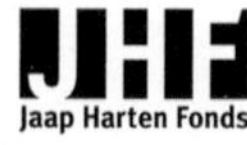 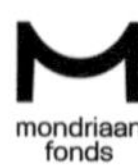 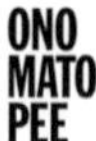

www.onomatopee.net

ISBN: 978-94-93148-98-7